Just Stop Motivating Me

Gavin Freeman

NEW
HOLLAND

CONTENTS

Foreword

Thank goodness someone wrote this book!

– Dan Gregory, CEO, The Impossible Institute

When Gavin Freeman asked me to write the foreword to the book you're currently holding in your hands, my response was, 'Thank goodness'.

In my opinion, much of what is referred to as "self-help" is in fact, not particularly helpful at all. Partly because it has us engage with an often well meaning fantasy that is highly intoxicating, but also prevents us from looking reality in the face and driving genuine and tangible progress.

In other words, there is a lot of motivational smoke being blown up our collective backsides and this needs to stop!

Much of this motivational hype is built on empty platitudes and very tantalising lies like, 'You can be anything you want to be'. Which is not to say that we can't have a significant impact in our own lives and indeed in the lives of others, it's just that such a statement is not particularly empowering if you don't entirely understand how you might fulfill these bold ambitions.

Many of these pithy platitudes have us banking on unrealistic expectations and using hope as a strategy. Certainly hope can be useful when that's all you're left with, but real motivation and personal engagement needs to be anchored more firmly in real strategies that can make a concrete difference.

I've spent most of my business career studying human behaviour and psychology: What drives us? What drives our teams and our customers? And what drives progress that is deliberate, consistent and congruent? Again and again, the message that we are bombarded with is that it all comes down to discipline and motivation. Of course, the problem with these twin strategies is that are only ever short term – no one is disciplined all of the time and certainly no one is motivated in every area of their life.

Recently, the business world has added another desired character attribute to discipline and motivation – resilience.

Which really translates to 'Just suck it up for another 9 yards ...' (Then, of course, we'll ask you to suck it up again.) This becomes another short-term solution that ultimately sets us up for exhaustion and failure.

The truth is: if you want to drive lasting change, design beats discipline. We need strategic leadership that leans more heavily on our systems and processes than on our people.

One of the critical mistakes we make in business, and even in our personal lives, is that we add layers of friction to processes that are anything but humanly intuitive and then get angry when we, or our staff, or customers, experience frustration or even rebel.

In other words, we make success more difficult and blame the human factor when a lack of strategy is a more likely culprit.

Better to work with who we, and they, really are not just who we would like them to be.

Over the years, I've had the privilege of working with Gavin in a number of different roles – each helping organisations navigate large scale cultural and market changes.

What I love about Gavin's work is that he's willing to face what's real and challenge popular wisdom with some scientific and psychological research. His work is quite the opposite of the empty promises of the self-help industry and is based on some extraordinary results he has achieved in the lives and businesses of his clients.

My suggestion is not to read this book as a means to bolstering your mindset, or lifting your mood, or even adding some extra hype to your already over-stimulated life, but rather to see it as a workbook. This is a practical guide to how success is achieved in the real world. A how-to that will help you navigate the realities of life but more importantly, realise true results.

Hopefully this is a sufficiently demotivating foreword for this exceptional little book. Because, we don't need more motivation, we need more of what Gavin's cooking ...

Dan Gregory CEO
The Impossible Institute
Gruen Transfer Panelist

ACKNOWLEDGEMENTS

Fi, my sleeping rock – no you don't! Thank you. Without you none of this would ever had been possible.

Jordy my darling – grow, challenge, explore and never ever give up.

Cody my little man – always be yourself, unless you can be batman, then always be batman.

Part I

INTRODUCTION

Where do you start a book on motivation, a topic that is so broad that it can easily be viewed from a variety of angles, perspectives and opinions? From early childhood, the driving force that stimulated people's actions and behaviours and what fuelled their insatiable desire and demand for improvement has always fascinated me. As I watch my children grow I am continually awestruck by the beauty and magic of their development and in some cases their similarities to me. But, on other occasions I question their parentage. One of my most incredible memories was watching my first born, only six years old at the time, run up and down the basketball court, negotiating what must have been the most confusing moment in her life. She had come face to face with what I considered to be the first of many situations that she would encounter in life that would require the motivation to act. What really happened though, was that the perception of the event combined with her own young biases and plans, created a motivational conundrum which I hope this book will describe.

At the tender age of six my daughter's reference point on interaction with the outside world was limited to her parents, grandparents and a sprinkling of family friends she had grown to love and admire. Now, there she was on a basketball court with her team of four other seven-year-olds (some that were already seasoned players), facing off against five other fresh-faced kids, being instructed by her coach to protect the ball at all costs. She had to work with these random little strangers, whose names she didn't know (sound familiar?). Her instructions were to dribble the ball to the end of the court (follow a strategy) and try to shoot it through the hoop (deliver on the strategy), while at the same time not allowing the opposition to get control of the ball (protect your IP and market share). She later described this instruction to me as 'Dad, they told me I am not allowed to share the ball with the other team' (ironically one of them was a friend from school). In fact, she was given additional instructions to "steal" the ball away from them, without being caught touching (fouling) them. Oh and to top it all off, mum and dad are sitting on the side, yelling their support for all these odd behavioural requests.

It would have been great if I could actually read minds and understood what she was thinking as she ran up and down the court, trying her best to figure out the rules of this strange game and carrying out the demands of her coach, with the vociferous encouragement of her family. To her credit she played the whole game with a smile on her face. But, she did hit me with the big question afterwards about why we always told her to share and now we were telling her to steal – out of the mouth of babes. She scored two points that game, and she and her team went on to win the league.

I bet you are wondering how I motivated her to play so well – and win – well you bought the book, so I will share my unique and amazing insights over the next couple of pages with you. I will guarantee that when you have finished reading this book you will be inspired and motivated. What I can't tell you though, is **what** you will be motivated to do.

So let's start. I sincerely hope you are prepared for what is about to happen as you delve into the unknown and become completely motivated to achieve something.

To get us started, have a think about a task that you haven't been overly motivated to complete. It could be a physical task like going for a run or doing some exercise, or a more cognitive based activity like having that tough conversation you have been avoiding.

The next few pages will change your perception of motivation, so much so, that if you don't burst out of your bubble by the end of it, I will personally refund you the purchase price. Minus, of course a fair amount for wear and tear, postage and handling, and of course GST.

Let's Start ...

Dig deep, I know you have the potential to achieve your goals.

Nope? Don't stress, just turn the page.

You miss a 100 per cent of the shots you don't take.

If that doesn't work, turn over the page.

If it's not hurting, you're not trying hard enough.

Seriously that must be working, but feel free to turn the page anyway.

There is no try! There is only do!

If that didn't work, you'll need to say it again with a Yoda voice this time.

If you just try a little harder you will be surprised at what you can achieve.

If I am still not getting through to you – it must be you.

Never give up, feel the burn!

Is it working yet?

I think I know what you are thinking right now!

Turn over to the next page.

Would you just stop motivating me!

This book has been written for you to explore the concept of motivation from a different point of view and for the consideration of alternate approaches. The aim is for you to understand not only what motivates you, but also what motivates others and how we can inspire them to achieve greatness. The basic principle of this concept is that it is time to stop motivating people and focus on creating an environment in which they choose to motivate themselves.

Chapter One

What is Motivation?

H ere we are, first chapter in and I am not sure that I have accomplished anything apart from amusing or irritating you. So, let's cut to the chase, we face a major problem with motivation and it's called – individualism. The reality is that we are all different, so for some, those words of encouragement may have stirred a burning desire to hit the gym or pound the pavement. But, for others they meant nothing and left them no more or less motivated than before. The second major problem that we face is that even those who felt the burning desire to conquer their mountain may wake up tomorrow and have a totally different mindset. Those same words that motivated them yesterday will now have little or no effect or importance. The opposite is also true – words of encouragement can be enhanced if we start to associate those words with something or someone more meaningful.

I will address these two problems in the upcoming chapters and will explain and ultimately propose alternate solutions and processes for your consideration.

So why is motivation so important? Not surprisingly, the theory of motivation is within our ability to understand, and has changed dramatically over time. However, our understanding of the concept has developed significantly over the last 20 years. It was unimaginable two decades ago that people would continuously volunteer their time, effort and resources to maintain a worldwide database of information for free. If I were bold enough to suggest that then, you likely would have suggested that I go back to school and reconsider my job as a consultant psychologist. In fact, you probably would have gone as far as to say that no one would ever do anything unless there was a very tangible and large reward attached to that work effort.

In his now famous TED talk, author Dan Pink provided an excellent example of the theory of motivation when he used the story of the phoenix, a legendary bird that was reborn into a new life as a result of rising from the ashes of its forerunner. In his analogy, Pink likened Encarta (Microsoft's online encyclopaedia – that had in fact taken over from *World Book*) to the ashes and Wikipedia to the Phoenix. In essence, he was suggesting that Wikipedia, the phoenix, dynamically rose and succeeded out of the ashes of its predecessor Encarta.

Ironically, I used Wikipedia to search for information on Encarta and found the following insert:

> **Microsoft Encarta** *was a digital multimedia encyclopaedia that was published by Microsoft Corporation from 1993 to 2009. In 2008, the complete English version, Encarta Premium, consisted of more than 62,000 articles. In March 2009, Microsoft announced it was discontinuing the Encarta disc and online versions. The MSN Encarta site was closed on October 31, 2009 in all countries except Japan, where it was closed on December 31, 2009.*
>
> "Encarta" – Wikipedia, the free encyclopaedia. Wikipedia.

Wikipedia, on the other hand, was started in 2001 and by 2015 the English Version had over 4.8 million articles and over 69,000 active editors – none of whom were paid. It is amazing to consider how a community of people from around the world would all be self-driven and motivated enough to contribute to a site, knowing perfectly well that others would be able to correct, amend or even disagree with their contribution. There is no other way to describe it than the perfect storm of a group of people who are simply motivated to succeed – but more on this concept later.

But could this just be a one off event, never to be repeated? Will it stand alone as a beacon of what could have been? The answer is no! Linux, a computer operating system based on the original Unix design, is an open source system that is available to the world gratis. While the provision of free source software is well documented in the literature, what is unique to Linux and other like systems is that they are continually maintained and updates are provided frequently. To test this, I loaded Linux onto an old laptop and the ease in which it worked, as well as the free support provided through various online forums, made the integration of the computer into my lifestyle effortless. Since installing the software it has continued to receive updates and appears to work as well, if not better than some of the other commercial operating systems available.

So the question is **why are people motivated to work** in this fashion and more importantly how can we understand it? We then need to consider the environment we work in and hopefully apply a different lens to how we drive our people and run our companies.

Much of what we know about motivation comes from years and years of academic research. Researchers have painstakingly tried to understand the concept, while developing theories that can then be applied in the real world. The problem research faces, is that for the most part it is either historical, that is we examine past behaviour and attempt to understand it. Or it is experimental; in which case we create an experiment in a lab (i.e. perfect conditions minus assumed assumptions) based on a hypothesis and again then interprets the results in order to make some sense of the data. While I am a scientist at heart and believe we need to conduct research to understand, I am also a realist and recognise that we will never truly know what is going on in someone's mind, and I don't believe we will ever find a way of measuring a 'mind'.

That being said, researchers have given us some insights into why people do the things they do and they have followed our journey from cave people to Wikipedia.

The next section will briefly explore the academic research to date, so that we can at least understand the background and place the proposition of this book in context.

ACADEMIC RESEARCH
The theories of motivation

I've named this section 'The theories of motivation' despite the fact that there is simply no way I can cover off, or even scratch the surface of the vast amount of literature out there on the topic. So being motivated to succeed, I have simply decided that they are all incorrect.

Well to be fair that is actually not quite the case, I believe that all theories are all just a little bit correct and incorrect, due to the fact that every theory ever researched always comes with a set of assumptions, which, if held true would validate the theory. The second issue that appears in the literature is that all the theories maintain that they can explain motivation and usually demonstrate why their approach is more valid than a previous approach. Hence, the argument that the next theory will supersede the most current one is born. So, which one is correct?

There is a place for each theory as they provide a perspective on the concept of motivation. When viewed independently they appear to be valid, however, when all the theories are viewed in line with each other, they start to reveal gaps in our understanding. I am in no way suggesting that my proposed theory on motivation is unique or more valid than any of the ones presented in this section of the book, I am simply proposing an alternative viewpoint for your consideration. In fact, I would recommend that you use all the theories to try to understand your own situation and then determine the best approach for you to achieve your specific goals. For every ten people who prove the theory, there is always one that does not.

With that in mind, I have a collection of some of the most prevalent theories on motivation, in what I like to refer to as 100 years of literature in one chapter.

Maslow's Hierarchy of needs

Many years ago, Abraham Maslow, an American psychologist, defined his needs-based model, suggesting that the basic level of needs should be met before we can move onto the next level. Maslow created the original five-level 'hierarchy of needs' model. The fifth level was originally referred to as 'self-actualising'. Later theorists have expanded the definition of self-actualisation and attempted to prioritise the levels. The additional three layers in the diagram below appear to simply be a more in-depth explanation of self-actualisation. In the current day and age the additional information is useful since as a society, we are becoming more aware of our self-actualising needs.

Maslow said that needs must be satisfied in the given order and that aims and drive always shift to the next higher order needs. Levels 1 to 4 are deficiency motivators, Level 5 and by implication 6 to 8 are growth motivators. The thwarting of needs is usually a cause of stress and is particularly so at Level 4.

23

FIGURE 1 MASLOW'S HIERARCHY OF NEEDS

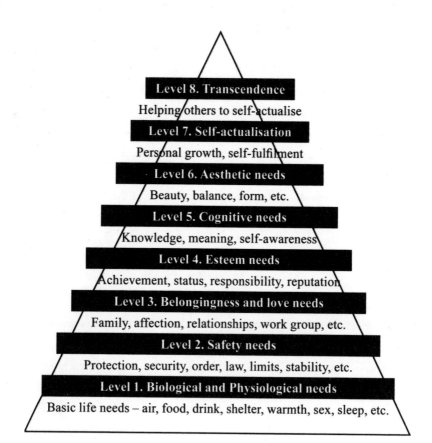

We could argue that our motivations are drawn from where we currently find ourselves in the hierarchy. The theory unfortunately falls short when we try to use it to explain the Wikipedia concept, as you could argue that some people may determine that some levels are more important than those below. Consider WikiLeaks and its founder Julian Assange who openly places his own safety at risk to achieve a higher goal. The same could be said about Edward Snowden.

Positive and Negative Reinforcement

Positive and negative theories of motivation stem from the original work presented by Maslow through his hierarchy of needs. The theory suggests that when an individual receives positive reinforcement that a particular behaviour will be continued. While it further suggests that when the same individual receives negative feedback they are likely to cease that behaviour. While on the surface this theory makes sense, in light of the motivational continuum presented in this book, it starts to fall short as individuals who are motivated to avoid failure may actually respond poorly to positive re-enforcement and vice versa. We often refer to this theory as the carrot and stick approach. The image of two riders are often presented in the media to reflect this – one holding a carrot in front of a horse enticing it to move faster and the other whipping the horse, suggesting that it would receive more punishment if it didn't move faster.

Ego vs. Goal/Task Orientation

Ego and task orientation theory suggests that an underlying personality trait ultimately drives our motivation to carry out a task. The theory suggests that ego oriented individuals focus primarily on the outcome (winning), while those who are goal oriented focus on the task (the steps needed to win).

For ego oriented people, a goal of displaying superiority over others while competing, is sufficient to allow that person to adhere to the task despite any feelings of discomfort. The task-oriented person may set a personal goal, which is powerful enough to mediate the discomfort they experience. When no concrete goal is set, the length of time spent tolerating discomfort may decrease in the ego-oriented individual. People who are task oriented may develop alternative goals, which usually include personal best or skills improvement and therefore can tolerate the discomfort longer. The motivation to continue a task is ultimately dependent on which trait is more powerful and how you are able to manipulate your environment to achieve the desired outcome. On the surface, ego orientation is somewhat aligned to the motivation to avoid a failure mind-set, while goal orientation is aligned to the motivation to succeed. The fundamental difference is that this theory does not suggest that a continuum between the two exists. It simply suggests that you have strengths and a predilection for one trait over the other.

Intrinsic vs. Extrinsic

The highest form of motivation occurs when an individual is most self-determined in his or her motivation. When intrinsically motivated, activities are engaged in for the inherent aspects of the activity itself. Relative autonomy is key to understanding self-determined motivation. Research specifically cites that those who are self-determined have 'more interest, excitement, and confidence, which in turn is manifest both as enhanced performance, persistence and creativity …' than their counterparts. On the other hand, external motivation is created when an individual is subjected to overt and external sources of incentive. There is no specific insight into the type of external incentive and whether some elements are more powerful than others. The research suggests that an external source of motivation is still given its power by the individual, as they still determine the impact of the stimuli.

Research suggests a hierarchical model of intrinsic and extrinsic motivation, which integrates the concept of a continuum of motivation, with the notion that motivation is exhibited at three levels of generality. From broad to specific, these levels are global, contextual and situational. Global motivation is the most general over-arching level of the three and it is often related to the overall attitude when conducting any task or activity (consider getting out of bed in the morning). Contextual motivation refers to motivation in specific contexts. An accountant's motivation for his/her profession is an example of contextual motivation. Situational motivation is the most specific form of motivation and represents the driving force that inspires an individual at a particular moment or time, when he or she is participating in or demonstrating a skill or task.

Your level of motivation may alter depending on the level that is prominent.

THEORIES ON INSPIRATION

Inspiration has three main qualities

Psychologists Todd M. Thrash and Andrew J. Elliot have noted three core aspects of inspiration: evocation, transcendence and approach motivation. Firstly, inspiration is evoked spontaneously without intention. Secondly, inspiration is transcendent of our more animalistic and self-serving concerns and limitations. Such transcendence often involves a moment of clarity and awareness of new possibilities. As Thrash and Elliot noted, 'the heights of human motivation spring from the beauty and goodness that precede us and awaken us to better possibilities'. This moment of clarity is often vivid and can take the form of a grand vision, or a "seeing" of something one has not envisioned before but was probably always there. We sometimes refer to the light bulb moment or a flash of inspiration. Finally, inspiration involves approach motivation, in which the individual strives to achieve, express, or actualise a new idea or vision. Accordingly, inspiration involves both being inspired by something and then acting on that inspiration.

Inspired people share certain characteristics
Thrash and Elliot also developed the 'Inspiration Scale,' which measures the frequency with which a person experiences inspiration in their daily lives. They found that inspired people were more open to new experiences and reported more absorption in their tasks. "Openness to Experience" often came before inspiration, suggesting that those who are more open to inspiration are more likely to experience it. Additionally, they noted that inspired individuals were not more conscientious, supporting the view that inspiration is something that happens to you and is not willed. Inspired individuals also reported having a stronger drive to master their work but were less competitive, which makes sense if you think of competition as a non-transcendent desire to outperform competitors. Inspired people were more intrinsically motivated and less extrinsically motivated, variables that also strongly impact work performance. Furthermore, it was found that inspiration was least related to variables that involve agency or the enhancement of resources, again demonstrating the transcendent nature of inspiration. Therefore, what makes an object inspiring is its perceived subjective intrinsic value and not how much it is objectively worth or how attainable it is. Inspired people also reported higher levels of important psychological resources, including belief in their own abilities, self-esteem and optimism. Mastery of work, absorption, creativity, perceived competence, self-esteem and optimism were all consequences of inspiration, suggesting

that inspiration facilitates these important psychological resources. Interestingly, work mastery also came before inspiration, suggesting that inspiration is not purely passive but favours the prepared mind.

Another important, trigger of inspiration is exposure to inspiring managers, role models, and heroes. As Gregory Dess and Joseph Picken noted in Changing Roles: Leadership In The 21st Century, 'Our competitive global economy requires leaders to shift their focus from efficient management to effective utilisation of a company's diversity of resources'. They argue for five key roles of inspiring leaders:

1. Using strategic vision to motivate and inspire
2. Empowering employees at all levels
3. Accumulating and sharing internal knowledge
4. Gathering and integrating external information
5. Challenging the status quo and enabling creativity

The theory, which appears on the surface to support my 'Just stop motivating me' theory, is the Self Determined Theory (SDT). SDT is a theoretical approach to an individual's motivation that gained increasing attention in organisational behaviour literature. The theory states that individuals have psychological needs for autonomy, competence and relatedness, which, if satisfied, may allow them to meet different goals. This model has its own principle in the dialectic vision between the efforts individuals make to satisfy such needs and the extent to which the external environment is able to respond to them (support).

Research by Deci and Ryan suggested that the self-determined feeling is the perception of pro-activity, freedom and autonomy of action. A motivated action may either be self-determined or controlled. As long as it is self-determined, it is perceived as a choice without coercion and emerging from the self, that is to say, not driven by an external force. From this perspective, SDT contributes to overcoming the static conceptualisation of intrinsic and extrinsic motivation, but it theorises the existence of several types of motivation, with differences among them being explained by the level of autonomy and freedom associated with the behaviour. Self-determined behaviour refers to an intrinsically motivated action involving curiosity, exploration, impulse and interest toward the environment. Intrinsically motivated actions arise exclusively from a spontaneous pleasure to perform them. People are able to reach high motivation levels when they feel connected to others in a social environment, when they can act effectively within such an environment and when they act with a feeling of personal initiative. Thus, in the organisational environments where the needs satisfaction is encouraged, it is quite likely that employees experience intrinsic motivation and engage in self-determined behaviours.

As I am sure you have seen the different theories are all as unique as they are similar. Therefore I will leave it to you to consider how each theory plays a role in the context you are working, playing or simply considering.

Theories are great – but they must be applicable

Before we can understand the interaction between motivation and behaviour we need to first understand the way the brain operates. While I do not propose to be an expert on the workings of the human brain, I could argue that although we have been able to map its structure, we still do not have a clear picture on how it works and more importantly, why it drives us to act in certain ways.

To simplify the explanation and for the purpose of the argument, let's consider and accept that the brain has two ways of interpreting information; emotional interpretations and logical/cognitive ones. To better explain this, reflect on a time when even though you had all the facts that supported your decision to act in a particular way, you simply decided to do something completely different because it 'just felt right.' It is this distinction that I am referring to and will spend the next few paragraphs explaining.

OUR BRAINS

To completely understand the concept of motivation, we need to have fundamental knowledge of how the brain works and the variables that impact it. Although we do not know a lot about how the brain actually works, we have inferred a number of factors and agreed on some of them. For those who are interested, there is a vast amount of literature on this section and I encourage you to explore at your leisure. Furthermore, I welcome any and all interesting insights that would advance our understanding and perception of the way the brain works.

For the purpose of this book, I have split the brain into the emotional and cognitive components as opposed to the right and left side concept that is often depicted in other literature.

Our **emotional brain,** which is sometimes referred to as the limbic system, is the part of the brain believed to interpret our world and provide us with our emotional interpretation of said world. The fascinating characteristic of this part of the brain is firstly, that it has no propensity for language and secondly, that it is believed by many to be home to the decision making part of the human brain. I will be focusing on the first part of that sentence, although the second part does provide some interesting thinking when it comes to concept of a 'gut decision'. You know, the one when all the evidence suggests X and yet your gut is telling you Y. Recruiting is a wonderful example of this; when a candidate looks and reads perfectly for a position on paper, yet after interviewing them they just don't feel right for the job. Or when a role is given to individuals who don't meet the educational or experience criteria, but just have something about them that feels right.

Common literature often refers to a particular part of this emotional area of the brain called the amygdala. With the phrase an 'amygdala hijack' often used as an apt descriptor when an individual becomes emotional and uncontrollable despite all regular reasoning. The extreme of this can often be quite alarming, however it happens on a regular basis to all of us. Consider coming home late at night to an empty house, you walk in the door and hear a noise – your amygdala immediately responds and you potentially perceive the worst. Your body starts to prepare for this, with the fight or flight response (your heart beats faster, blood flows to the extremities and the adrenaline starts pumping), until you switch on the light and realise that the wind coming through the open window was blowing the curtains and the bang was simply the latch on the frame. Emergency averted, internal DEFCON rating reduced to zero and a fleeting moment of internal embarrassment is replaced with the sound of cork being removed from your favourite bottle of red.

The emotional part of our brain does not know how to interpret feelings, as by definition it simply feels them and allows the other part of our brain to interpret them, often incorrectly. Let's use another example. Consider these questions: Do you have a significant other? Do you have a family? Do you love them?

Assuming you answered in the affirmative …

WHY?

Trying to answer this question is fraught with danger, anything you say could have the potential to backfire (in the nicest possible way of course). The challenge here is that there is no answer. What you have been doing is creating a list in your head, which realistically can only be described as the features and benefits list. It's your cognitive brain attempting to interpret an emotion.

We do the same thing when we buy a new car. We select a car just because we like it, then we look at the list of inclusions and use them to rationalise the decision to buy the car and justify the expense to our partner.

The disconnect between language and emotion is a core concept which will be explored throughout the book, as it plays a fundamental role in understanding why people act the way they do. The final thought I will leave you with before moving on to the cognitive brain, is that our emotional brain is far more powerful than our logic brain – just try to argue the opposite! You can try but the comeback answer is always 'Yes, I agree, BUT ...'

Our **cognitive brain** is the part of the brain that is responsible for that features and benefits list previously discussed – remember the reasons you considered about why you loved your significant other. For the purpose of this book I am going to limit the description in this section as it can become very confusing.

The cognitive part of the brain is responsible for making sense of the world. It integrates all the information it receives and attempts to logically and succinctly create order. The challenge here is that the information we receive is not all equal, so it also has to develop a process for prioritising it. Remember when you considered the 'why' question around your loved ones, the answer you provided demonstrated this prioritisation process. It also did something unique, it considered your perspective and it also considered the information in the context in which it was given. This contextualisation process is probably the most important aspect of this section, as it plays a vital role in understanding the motivational mindset that is discussed in the next chapter. From a very early age we start to learn overtly and vicariously through others, what the most appropriate actions or behaviours are in particular circumstances. We don't talk during assembly, we stop when we hear a whistle, we recognise the tone in our parents' voices when they are grumpy and don't talk back. We are constantly bombarded with stimuli and our brain is in continual interpretation and reaction mode, so to speed up the process it begins to create shortcuts. We recognise elements of a situation and jump to a conclusion, simply because it is easier. It is this action which can both save our lives and impact on our motivation to act.

Let's consider the example of public speaking, which is used extensively throughout the book. Many of us recognise and will articulate that we are afraid and in some cases petrified of public speaking, but I wonder how many of you have the proof that it is that scary. How many people have actually stood up in front of a thousand people and spoken? For many people, the fear of public speaking is the cognitive brain's interpretation of the emotional brain's sensation of fear, or the perceived outcome of the event. We experience the sensation that is described as fear and then we try to interpret it. While I am not saying that everyone can be an amazing public speaker through accurate interpretation, I am suggesting that we may not be using the best interpreter. Our cognitive brain is a wonderful tool and can compute decisions at a million miles an hour yet struggles to interpret emotions.

Another aspect of the cognitive brain that is particularly noteworthy for this book is that it is essentially the yardstick used to measure one response compared to another. Through evolution, we have been able to develop our brain to complete a number of amazing tasks and one of them is the ability to evaluate two vastly different situations and somehow compare them on a comparable platform. Well that is the theory anyway.

So when we are placed in a situation in which we are forced to compare these two similar, but often very different variables, how do we do it? Continuing with the public speaking example, while many would argue that they are fearful of speaking in public, most will concede that they are able to speak to their friends; some would even suggest that speaking at a party is fine; a couple more might say that a discussion at work over a project is still OK and a few may even go so far as to say that a presentation to their manager is fine. 'But no way could I ever speak in front of a large audience' is what you often hear. The interesting truth is that the individual has probably never spoken in front of a large audience, so he/she is using a perceived 'yard stick' to measure their public speaking success. On the other hand they have often spoken at family functions, so in that case a reality based 'yard stick' is being used. The problem is that they are not the same 'yard sticks'. On the surface the public speaking is the same, however, in this case the context in which the speaking will occur is very different.

WHY WE MOTIVATE

Why is motivation so important? Who should be doing the motivating? The current viewpoint in 2015 is that organisations must not only provide the infrastructure (cyber and physical) to carry out work but also individualised motivation, so that every employee remains engaged, committed and applies discretionary effort to all tasks performed. In most cases to achieve this, organisations place a dollar value on KPI's (Key Performance Indicators) assigned to the role and then expect their managers to complete a learning plan, which apparently sets out the expected behaviours required to achieve the KPI's. Some companies go a step further and provide an additional opportunity to add extra motivation – a bonus. A bonus is an arbitrary figure that is decided on by an organisation that is deemed sufficient enough to motivate their employees to work that little bit harder and exceed the already determined KPI's. From the employee's perspective, they were asked to produce under one set of expectations and now they are given an extra, often referred to as a stretch goal, which will enable them to make a little more cash. Let's play this out – I am earning $100,000 to do an excellent job and now you are offering me an extra $10,000 (yep a whole 10 per cent) if I go above and beyond my regular, excellent job. If I do my work, I get the 100k but if I flog myself, I am going to make an extra $10k. But what if I flog myself and barely miss out – in some cases I might get some of my bonus or possibly none at all! Now I am left with a decision do I or don't I? If I just simply turn up, I still get the $100k.

For what it is worth, why not ensure that I am the best person for the job; pay me $110,000 dollars and set very clear and achievable expectations. The chance you take is that the extra $10k may actually have the reverse effect on my motivation, especially if the goal is too high and unachievable or if there is no process by which I can influence the outcome (consider all the admin roles or non-income producing roles whose bonuses are tied to the company's performance. How can they control the way that their performace is evaluated?). In the face of perceived failure, we often alter our behaviour and demonstrate characteristics unlike anything we have ever shown before (but more of this in chapter 2).

Consider if you have ever experienced a decrease in motivation as a result of a bonus goal being set too far out of reach. It is my belief that motivation can only come from within and that we can drive ourselves to achieve amazing results. However, our ability to drive others is person-dependent and usually short lived when delivered without a sense of inspiration.

The following chapters will explore our motivational mindset and provide a deeper insight into the concept of motivation and how we can inspire others to achieve greatness. It is my goal to provide you with enough evidence to stop you from motivating others and focus on processes by which they can control their own destiny and you yours.

Your role in this book is to challenge your own motivational paradigm. Einstein once said that the conscious mind that identifies a problem cannot solve it. And this is even truer when it comes to self-motivation and the inspiration of others. If we know how to drive ourselves further, why aren't we just doing it? Yet we look to others and gasp in exhilaration when we see them achieving goals and outcomes, which we know we have the capacity for …

Chapter Two

The Motivational Mindset

I have missed more than 9,000 shots in my career
I have lost almost 300 games
Twenty-six times I have been trusted to take the game winning shot and missed
I have failed over and over and over again
And that is why I succeed

Michael Jordan.

I n the previous chapter I started to shift the thinking of motivation from a concept, whereby we influence the mindset of an individual and somehow create a sense of discretionary effort and a drive, which will continue once the stimulus, has been removed. This change of thought moves to a position in which the motivation of an individual's behaviour has to lie purely within but is determined by both their emotional and cognitive make up. This mindset will form the focus of the next chapter and I will present a perspective, which will guide the remainder of the book and provide you with an alternative viewpoint.

It is important to recognise that the stick theory (i.e. if I do something wrong I will receive a form of punishment and if I demonstrate the correct behaviour I will receive some reward) is still prevalent and in the armoury of many leaders. However I would argue that it is waning to the internal vs. external theory (if I believe in it I will continue to act in a particular way or if someone provides me with enough of an external incentive I may also choose to act in the same way). In reality neither of these theories help when we consider how society responds as a whole. Let's look for instance at law enforcement. We have laws with punishments attached to them for when they are broken, yet people continue to commit crimes. We have also tried to incentivise people for behaving in a certain way, yet again no consistency appears in the human condition therefore, we are always left with 'well it depends' or 'that person is just different'.

Malcolm Gladwell in his latest book *David and Goliath* explored this in more detail when considering the three strikes law in California, to determine whether it actually reduced the crime rate. The three strikes law was first introduced in 1993 and stated that an individual who had already committed two previous crimes would face significantly harsher penalties if they were convicted of a third crime, the sentence often ranging between 25 years and life imprisonment. On the surface, one could imagine that individuals would be motivated not to commit crimes or at least reduce their criminal behaviour after one or two strikes. Ironically, while the crime rate in California did drop somewhat after the three-strike law was entered into legislation, research has determined that the three strikes law actually had little or no effect on the deterrence of crime. The research concluded that the three strikes law was ineffective due to the diminishing marginal returns associated with each criminal. In real terms, this meant that those committing serious crimes were already locked up for extended periods of time (so they were technically out of the system). It didn't apply to juveniles and finally and more disturbingly, there was an increase in crimes committed against police officers, as criminals on their third strike would often retaliate against them to increase their chances of escape. A wide and disturbing trend was that many criminals who were punished under this law were fathers and members of communities. The net effect here was the perpetuation of future crimes by young children who grew up with absent fathers

This continuing trend, of trying to understand motivation only to become stuck when someone does not act in the way that the theory proposes, leads us to the motivational mindset. I am not proposing this continuum is a replacement for the current theories. I am suggesting however, that if used in conjunction with them, it will provide additional insight into our motivation to act and ultimately support our decision making from a personal as well as an external perspective.

The motivational mindset is a continuum that is as simple and elegant in its design and application, as it is complex and confusing. There is no right or wrong side, as we shift across the continuum depending on the environment we are in. The level of complexity becomes more apparent as we try to apply it to the population we are working with. The factors that move you from one side of the continuum to the other are very different and there is no broad stroke that will apply (which is why the three strikes law simply could never work).

The motivational mindset spans the continuum from a Motivation to Succeed (MTS) through to a Motivation to Avoid Failure (MTAF). It is presented on a continuum and not in a matrix like other theories for various reasons. The typical four-quadrant matrix, while useful for describing a number of reactions where you can increase or decrease a factor simply does not work in this situation. This is so, because the motivational mindset can change if the same behaviour is performed in different environments. Additionally, we are also likely to experience both sides of the continuum within the same activity if a small contextual change occurs. What this means is that an action or task can be performed within a motivation to succeed mindset in one context, whereas on the other hand that same task or action can easily shift the individual into a motivation to avoid failure mindset, with a simple change in context or environment.

Perhaps you may think that this all sounds very confusing but once we put some examples to the continuum it will all make absolute sense.

To circle back to the example of public speaking, research has shown us that a large proportion of the population would rather choose death than public speaking. Jerry Seinfeld captured it perfectly when he said:

> *According to most studies, people's number one fear is public speaking. Number two is death. Death is number two. Does that seem right? That means to the average person, if you have to go to a funeral, you're better off in the casket than doing the eulogy.*

If we believe this premise to be true, then we can now use the example to perfectly illustrate the continuum. On one side is the mindset of MTAF, and within the context of public speaking that makes perfect sense. You are asked to stand in front of a large crowd, maybe with a microphone attached to your lapel, the entire presentation being recorded for posterity while your head is displayed on a large screen highlighting every single 'um', 'ah' and 'eyes down' moment. Some of you may even experience a physical reaction (a panic attack) to that description but most could understand the mindset when under significant scrutiny like that, to be one of, 'I had better not stuff this one up, everyone will see me fail'. The negative evaluation of you by yourself and by others becomes overwhelming. It is important to remember that this reaction is driven when you are in the MTAF mindset.

Let's calm the situation down somewhat, you still have to make your presentation but now the context is a small working room in the corner of your office. It's a room you have been in many times before, there are no large screens, no lapel mikes and the only recording that may be happening is someone ignoring your presentation and watching the latest silly cat video on YouTube. The people in the room are members of your team and you feel completely comfortable speaking in front of them. Given this change in context one could easily slip across the continuum and into the MTS mindset. Here, a mistake would simply be met with either friendly banter or a note to fix that section in the presentation. You are likely to be highly engaged and focused on doing a good job as opposed to not making a mistake. You have also just shifted into the MTS mindset.

UNDERSTANDING THE MINDSETS

How do we know which mindset we are in and more importantly how do we recognise which side of the continuum our clients or staff are in?

The first part of the question is somewhat easier compared to the second part. To fully understand the continuum as it applies to you requires an opening up of your mind to both recognising and accepting your signs and symptoms. Once you have achieved this, you are well on your way to developing control over your motivational mindset and utilising it.

Motivation to Succeed

The MTS mindset is often characterised by individuals who are driven to achieve mastery over a task. They are intuitively involved in the process of achieving success and will understand the mechanics and the levers required to be successful. Through this they will be prepared, process focused, highly transparent and ethical and will not only focus on themselves, but also on their team achieving success. Individuals who work independently of a team will still focus on how their support team has contributed to the success. For the very few individuals who operate completely alone, I salute you but still maintain that you meet the first part of the statement. When we are in the MTS mindset we often display an AIM-FIRE-ADJUST perspective on effort. I like to refer to this as 'The Angry Birds Methodology'. Angry Birds is an incredibly successful App, which requires the user to break down a number of different structures using various birds who all have different characteristics. The game encourages you to keep trying each level over and over again to not only free the piggies but also complete the level in the most efficient way.

The angry birds methodology suggests that when presented with a challenge you need to break down the tasks required, understand the tools you have and fail fast and cheaply. It is the last component that truly captures the MTS mindset. The luxury of the angry bird game is that you get to try over and over again, each time learning from your mistakes, until you achieve the three stars of success. Failure in this game can be simply interpreted as a stepping stone to future success. This stepping stone mentality is fundamental to the MTS mindset, without it, it's a slippery slope to the MTAF mindset. The thinking process requires you to AIM and make some strategic decisions, FIRE and evaluate the outcome and finally ADJUST to improve on your past performance (AIM-FIRE-ADJUST). This process is somewhat different when we are in the MTAF mindset, which is best characterised by AIM-ADJUST-ADJUST-ADJUST … FIRE (maybe – but more on this later in the chapter). Before we discuss the other side of the continuum, it is important to recognise that when we are in the MTS mindset we perceive failure very differently to when we are in the MTAF mindset. While the angry birds methodology points out the behavioural components of the mindset, there are some associated thoughts to consider.

Perceiving Failure in the MTS Mindset

When in the MTS mindset, we perceive actual failure or even the imminence of failure, we start to behave in a particular way.

We redirect and increase our effort and intensity. Practically, we try harder by at times just doing the same thing over and over again and expecting a different result (often referred to as insanity). We stop and reset our focus if required. Under pressure and during stress we can often unknowingly shift our focal point and narrow down on the wrong aspect. This could be an actual focal point (something realistic) or it could be an emotional focus (a thought). Failing is a great opportunity to check in and ensure that we are focusing on the best possible aspects of the task. We take ownership of the error, which is probably the most profound aspect of this mindset. Openly verbalising that we have made a mistake and then most importantly highlighting what we plan to do to amend it, ensures that we remain accountable to the task and also enhances the likelihood of success. This allows us to refocus and where possible bring alternative perspectives into the mix. You won't be surprised to learn that when we openly discuss a concept and tacitly give others permission to contribute – they do! Finally, in line with the commentary already discussed, we simply see failure as a stepping stone to success.

The image below captures it all in a succinct manner.

Motivation to succeed mindset

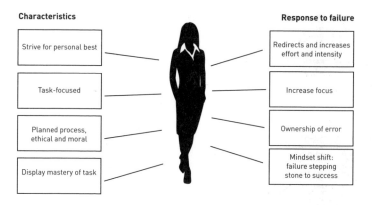

Motivation to Avoid Failure

The MTAF mindset is a completely different set of steak knives, but there is one distinct common thread, which needs to be highlighted. This motivational mindset continuum is unique, in that while it explains reactions to success and failure, it does not have the outcome of failure at its core. What I mean by this is that when we are in the MTAF mindset we still want to succeed, we just go about it in a different way. The underlying psychology in this mindset is vastly dissimilar. Fear of failure is a very powerful emotion and the driver of behaviour. Individuals when in this mindset often don't realise that they are failing until it becomes very obvious or they are caught. Lance Armstrong the disgraced cyclist is a sad but perfect example. To the world he was a champion, winning numerous races, overcoming a major illness and achieving accolades most of us can only dream of – and then he was caught. On the surface all we saw was success after success but we now know that all of this success came off the back of a MTAF mindset, which drove him to ensure his success by cheating. The difficulty with this mindset is that had he not been caught we would never have known. The MTAF mindset is activated when the context or the environment becomes such, that the fear of failing overrides our drive to achieve personal mastery. Failure in this mindset can be either likely or imminent, or it could be less overt and characterised by 'I simply don't have enough information to ensure my success'.

The MTAF mindset has a number of unique characteristics to identify when you are in this side of the continuum. Individuals will feel the need to display superiority over others and will want to achieve at any cost. This can sometimes be misinterpreted as assertive or aggressive type behaviour, but it is simply a need to ensure they are being successful as the fear of failing is overwhelming. The MTAF mindset has an ingenious way though, of trying to protect itself, I like to refer to it as the 'I haven't studied for this one' characteristic. What this is referring to is the behaviour in which an individual even prior to starting an activity (success or failure is not even a factor yet) pre-empts the possibility of failure and inserts the excuse mechanism early. We all remember a time when walking into an exam 'our friend' turned to us and said 'I haven't studied for this one'. Then two weeks later after finding out the results, would either refer to the earlier statement and comment, 'See I told you I would fail as I hadn't studied' – minimising or even removing the interpretation of failure – or in absolute jubilation says, 'I am a genius, nailed the exam without even studying' – further reinforcing their superiority over others mindset. Angry birds also play a role in helping define the MTAF mindset. In the MTS mindset you use the AIM-FIRE-

ADJUST approach. The MTAF mindset restructures that approach into AIM-ADJUST-ADJUST... FIRE (maybe). Consider the classic example of being asked to come up with a new innovative way of achieving a goal. In this mindset you will still aim at the goal, but you come unstuck as you start to adjust. The reason for multiple adjustments is because you never feel like you will actually succeed. So instead of trying (FIRE) you procrastinate in the adjustment phase and often when you do fire it is too late and you have missed the boat. The concept of learning from our mistakes is not new; in fact it is well researched both anecdotally and scientifically. We all started in this mindset as children, while receiving that wonderful message from our parents, 'Just try – it doesn't matter if you fail, you just need to have a go'. This phrase and others like it were often heard on the playground, in the study or heading into the drama auditorium. For some reason, this message starts to become a little cloudy when we enter high school and even more so during our post school education. Later on in life, we begin to hear a different message 'don't fail or you won't be able to get into a certain career or stream and ultimately be successful in life'.

A colleague and business partner once described this as the JFDI principle – but to keep some mystery I will let you try and work that one out for yourself (Clue the F is what you think it is!)

I am not blaming the school system, I'm simply trying to highlight the impact of society on our motivation mindset. Children learn very quickly the benefits of success and the perils of failure, which have ultimately created the other side of the continuum. The continual adjustment is usually a reflection of your own inner doubt. This could be extrapolated as 'They would never accept this' and internalised as 'I am not good enough'. Had I been in this (MTAF) mindset, this book may never have been written. Imagine me, sitting in my office, thinking I had a great idea for a book, only to become stuck in the adjust mindst of 'No publisher will print it' or worse 'No one will buy it, so why bother?'.

There is one additional characteristic, which is contrary to the ones mentioned above and often provides a conundrum to leaders when trying to understand and explain someone's behaviour. The characteristic is one defined by withdrawal and striving for mediocrity. This characteristic is on the surface perplexing as it does not appear to align at all with the 'need to display superiority over others' or 'achievement at any cost'. It is however perfectly aligned, as when you think slightly deeper into the psyche of someone who is motivated to avoid failure, it becomes clear that they may choose to actually never place themselves in a situation whereby they could even be evaluated at all. Consider the perspective of 'If I just do enough to fly in under the radar, I will never be singled out, evaluated and likely never have to experience the situation of being negatively evaluated'. They would never volunteer for a new project or offer up an opinion in an innovation workshop or the like. But what they would do is volunteer to take on a task that is guaranteed to fail. The reasoning is that when the outcome of failure is expected then all efforts towards trying to achieve success will be deemed favourably.

Perceiving Failure in the MTAF Mindset

Our emotional brain is continually evaluating the world we are in and providing us with a constant stream of feelings. The feeling of failure is quite universal and is often associated with a number of negative thoughts (best for you to consider your own here as the list would be too long if I tried to capture them all). While it is good to understand the negative thoughts we have, they don't go far enough to help understand this side of the continuum. Here, we need to look for behaviours as a better source of insight into the impact of a fear based mindset. When we perceive failure, the tendency is to not explore the feeling but rather consider the impact. A boxer getting into the ring and eyeing a more formidable opponent may start to consider the pain associated with being struck, a salesperson may consider the impact of not landing a new client and their ability to support their family. The outcome of this interpretation may then drive a change in behaviour, which will be very different when you are in the MTAF mindset. In this mindset, they are more likely to stray away from the original plan and attempt to protect their ego. Not only are you likely to forego the plan you had but you are also likely to forget all the training you have done and previous recollections of when you were in this situation and able to work your way out of it. The main thought process is 'I need to protect myself'. Unfortunately, many of our actions are further reinforced when we receive more overt indicators of failure. The boxer may experience pain with the first punch to make contact, while the sales person may interpret a lack of interest in the prospective client, when they do not maintain eye contact or choose to check an email on their phone. The brain may perceive this as a self- fulfilling prophecy and ultimately enhance the negative blowback the individual will experience. Unfortunately, we are not always aware of this and do not recognise our mindset position until the behaviours become more prevalent.

Let's explore this in greater detail in a workplace context. Think of an individual who is in the MTAF mindset and is walking into an important internal meeting. The individual may start to consider the outcome if they say or suggest something that could be perceived as incorrect. They start to overanalyse the situation and end up convincing themselves that if they say something incorrect, it would be a career limiting move and affect their promotional opportunities. The outcome in the individuals mind is that they err on the side of caution and choose not to contribute to the meeting. In this example, there was no failure but success was also left wanting. The manager on the other hand may have interpreted it differently, assuming the person is not vested in the topic or department and not a team player.

Let's explore another situation with a slightly different outcome. The same meeting but this time the individual chooses to contribute to the discussion, however, their perspective is not met with the same level of enthusiasm in which it was delivered. I was recently coaching a young executive who was charged with presenting a proposal on which concept they would recommend the organisation adopt as a national approach. The person had recently taken on the role and would have been the first to agree that he was not the expert in the field. His team collated the numbers and a final position was developed. Here is where I deviate from what really happened, but let's assume that the individual went into the meeting and presented that data and the proposed approach and the CEO (who knew the business inside and out) found a mistake in the calculations. The MTAF mindset would have shifted into over-drive and resulted in the individual defining and protecting their position by deferring the blame to others or even excusing the mistake due to their lack of experience. Either way, the goal shifted from a company focus to a self-protection focus.

I have always wondered what the mindset of a barrister is when they realise they are going to lose, or more emotionally, the mindset of a soldier when there is no hope of getting out of the situation alive.

What we do know is that there are a number of characteristics that are common in this mindset and very prevalent when failure is imminent or expected.

The assumption here is that the brain has shifted from a success perspective, to an ego protection perspective.

We blame, justify, defend and deny, the good old 'BJDD'.

Blame is a wonderful tool in which we can extrapolate the excuse of failure to someone or something else. Using the earlier example, 'I made a decision based on the numbers I had, if they were wrong or misinterpreted by my team then I cannot be blamed for coming to this conclusion'. Blaming is easy especially if the person being blamed is not in the room or even better if it's an object. I really feel sorry for golf clubs and software codes. As a collective group they must need some serious counselling to cope with all the blame they receive in absentia.

Justifying is a smaller version of blame but not as harsh. We can justify our behaviour in a number of ways; 'I didn't have enough time, resources etc. to achieve the desired outcome'. We often use justification when we want to blame someone or something but just don't have enough evidence to make it stick. It's a softer approach but still protects the ego.

Defending, on the other hand is very different, in this mindset we protect our position by starting the sentence with, 'I agree with you, but' or 'Yes, but'. The 'but' is the transition into the deflecting of any negative evaluation by initially agreeing an error occurred but then inferring that you couldn't be held accountable for it. The fundamental difference between this protection mechanism and the justification is that you partially agree there was a mistake – it may be semantics but they are different. The final piece is the flat out denial. I couldn't resist but I like to refer to this as the Shaggy approach 'It wasn't me'. For those not old enough to understand the reference, head to YouTube and search for the song by Shaggy called 'It wasn't me'. The theme of the song was to simply deny any wrong doing regardless of how much evidence was piling up. Denial is a powerful tool in our armoury and when delivered convincingly, it may not only lead the perpetrator of the negative evaluation to change their perspective, but if powerful enough, it can actually distort the reality of the individual, leaving them in a position in which they start to believe their own rhetoric. Neither situation is useful as the outcome is unlikely to ever achieve its desired status and the individual will quite frankly never develop.

Some other responses to failure when in this mindset include the increase in cheating, which now explains the Lance Armstrong situation. He chose to cheat to protect his ego and it wasn't until he was caught that it all made sense. Cheating in the workplace can also be experienced as stealing – consider how you felt when a colleague stole your idea and pitched it as their own. The final piece of the behavioural puzzle is the paradoxical decrease in effort and intensity. On the surface this doesn't make any sense but given the argument provided above, one could very easily make the connection between effort and intensity and the statement, 'I would have been successful but I just didn't try hard enough'. We often see this in young kids who give up when they receive negative feedback but it is just as prevalent in the corporate environment. Individuals stop trying and create a paper trail of excuses to be summoned at a moments notice.

Motivation to avoid failure mindset

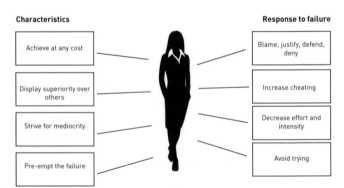

Chapter Three

Good to Great

A n article written by business consultant and academic, Jim Collins in 2001 started like this.

I want to give you a lobotomy about change. I want you to forget everything you've ever learned about what it takes to create great results. I want you to realise that nearly all operating prescriptions for creating large-scale corporate change are nothing but myths.

In the business world, we operate within a reality that is grounded by the business, newspaper or website you visited this morning, but is driven by the various myths that have circled around for years and like the mythical beasts whose stories have scared children for umpteen years, only the names and faces are changed. Jim refers to a number of specific myths including The Myth of the Burning Platform, which suggests employees are so unmotivated that they need something to be on fire just for it to gain their attention; The Myth of Stock Options, which suggests that there is no problem that can't be fixed by throwing more money at it; The Myth of Fear-Driven Change, which suggests that scaring people into making change is the best way to achieve the change required; and The Myth of Technology-Driven Change, which suggests that technology is the key to changes in the future. This works on the understanding that clearly only some new amazing technology will help us overcome the competition.

Jim summarises his thoughts as follows.

> *Here are the facts of life about these and other change myths. Companies that make the change from good to great have no name for their transformation – and absolutely no program. They neither rant nor rave about a crisis – and they don't manufacture one where none exists. They don't "motivate" people – their people are self-motivated. There's no evidence of a connection between money and change mastery. And fear doesn't drive change – but it does perpetuate mediocrity. Nor can acquisitions provide a stimulus for greatness: Two mediocrities never make one great company. Technology is certainly important – but it comes into play only after change has already begun. And as for the final myth, dramatic results do not come from dramatic process – not if you want them to last, anyway. A serious revolution, one that feels like a revolution to those going through it, is highly unlikely to bring about a sustainable leap from being good to being great.*

What is great about this article is that the concept of motivation coming from within and not from management was already starting to formulate. In this chapter I will expand on this concept and suggest the next step forward in the evolution of the thinking around greatness but from the perspective of motivation. The previous chapters have created an argument that motivation sits on a continuum and is not linear in its approach. If we are to accept that as the truth, then we also need to consider that greatness is also on a continuum and not necessarily linear. We do not develop greatness by first starting at being average and then progressing through being good and so on. This methodology is completely accurate when it comes to skills and learnt skills but when it comes to greatness from a motivational sense it simply cannot apply. Consider this scenario, a surgeon who has spent hundreds of hours honing their skills, reading textbooks, watching surgeries, performing minor procedures with someone observing; or a pilot who has progressed from learning how to fly a Cessna to sitting in the cockpit of a Boeing 747 200B after countless hours in the simulator and thousands of hours flying time. Now let's determine their greatness and their motivation to perform.

> *It's 2 a.m. and sirens are wailing, the paramedic rushes through the door with a severely injured person on the gurney, at the same hour, a Boeing 747 is flying over the Pacific Ocean having said goodbye to air traffic control and settling in for a long haul flight the pilot notices a number of indicator lights and sirens starting to blare.*
>
> *The sirens are blaring for both individuals, lights are flashing, people are screaming – the reality of the situation is quickly becoming clear. Flames leap from the engine of the 747, as the US President sleeps on Air Force One, while the surgeon looks down and the Prime Minister is on the table.*

Just your average day for both individuals, but I would argue that it is in this moment that we truly experience the difference between good and great and understand how these individuals are actually motivated to succeed and not motivated to avoid failure. Individuals who are good are by definition can perform the skills required to be deemed and evaluated as competent. They understand the implications of the role and can articulate in an interview why they would be successful in gaining a similar position elsewhere. What the above situation requires though, is more than good. It requires greatness and by my definition the difference between good and great is:

The ability to perform consistently under pressure.

This ability is the natural next step in the evolution of the argument. It is no longer good enough to just be good at your job. We have to be able to perform our roles at the same standard, regardless of the pressures being exerted on us. For all the armchair sport coaches out there, you will understand the frustration of watching your team perform well one week and awfully the next. Commentators often refer to this as consistency but in reality it is simply a team that is good but not great. Greatness in this capacity can be developed, and while education is an important start, we need to consider the formula for greatness and then consider how we are creating an environment that will foster the motivation for greatness. There are many great pilots and surgeons out there but I am not convinced that all of them would willingly relish the opportunity faced in the example given above and be motivated to volunteer. It is our motivation to perform, which forms the backbone of our ability to be great but motivation does not stand-alone. We need to have the behavioural experience and cognitive understanding to be able to truly perform consistently under pressure.

Below is my formula for greatness which is underpinned by 3 elements – cognition, behaviour and motivational mindset. The following section will expand on how we can develop it.

Difference between good and great = f (Ability to perform consistently under pressure)
Cognitions   Behaviours   Motivation

Model of performing under pressure

Performing under pressure has at its core four key principles. All four principles inform the three key elements of the greatness formula. For example, resilience will impact on the way we think as well as the way we act and inform our motivation. So consider each principle, not as an individual factor but as a contributor to the entire formula. Each principle is affected by how our emotional brain perceives it, our logical brain interprets it, and our motivational mindset allows us to achieve it.

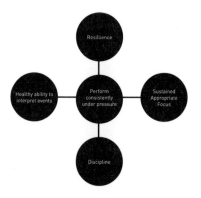

Resilience

Resilience is the ability to take a knock and bounce back, get off the ground, shake off the dirt and re-engage in the task or activity you were doing. All three elements play a role, when we feel like we cannot continue, our emotional brain feels defeated and a concept called emotional reasoning occurs – 'If I feel it, it must be true'. The cognitive brain misinterprets the sensation of defeat and interprets it in a way that suggests a never-ending pattern of failure is obvious, so you may as well give up. Resilient individuals understand this and force a correction. They re-interpret the situation and find the strength to continue. The most powerful tool you have is your motivation to succeed. Consider a time when you felt you might not have been as resilient as you would have liked, capture your thoughts in a book and consider the signs and symptoms you demonstrated. Recognising these signs in the future can be a useful start in building your resilience.

Sustained appropriate focus

We recognise that under pressure we often narrow our focus onto irrelevant stimuli or we completely lose it. Our ability to perform under pressure is directly related to the strength of our focal point. Having appropriate, transparent and achievable goals at the front of our mind will enable us to maintain the level of focus needed to be successful. If our goals are haphazard, unclear or not present, our ability to block out distractions and respond to failures is significantly reduced. The key here is not actually the word 'focus' but 'appropriate' as we can be focused on the wrong aspect. Driving while focused on your smart phone demonstrates focus, just not appropriate focus.

Discipline

It would be impossible to achieve anything in life if we did not have the discipline to stay the line. Consider how many New Year's resolutions were left stranded on the 2nd of January or how many sit-ups, push-ups or jogs around the neighbourhood have been missed in lieu of a muffin. Our ability to be motivated is directly influenced by our discipline to remain motivated. Remember, discipline is a state of mind, not a series of actions. We can fake actions for a period of time, but to be truly disciplined, we need to believe in our actions.

Healthy ability to interpret events

We need to recognise that bad situations do arise from time to time, we will not achieve every goal we set and our car is likely to get scratched in the parking lot. It is our motivational mindset that directly informs how our cognitive and emotional brain reacts to these situations. We have all yelled (overtly or covertly) at someone who cut us off in traffic or pushed in front of us in a line, but I wonder how often we catch ourselves in the moment and realise that we actually have a choice in how we are going to react. Assuming you are going to have a bad day is a great way of starting the day off with the glass half empty. I recall seeing a poster on social media, which went something like this.

A Harvard Professor of Psychology walked around a room full of students while teaching about stress management.

To begin his lecture he grabbed a glass of water and raised it above his head as if he was going to propose a toast, and instantly everyone expected they'd be asked if the glass was half empty or half full as part of the lesson. Instead though, with a smile on his face, the professor asked 'how heavy is this glass of water?'.

Students called out answers '6 ounces' and '10 ounces'

but he shrugged them off.

He replied, 'the actual weight doesn't matter. What really matters is how long I've been holding it. If I hold it for just a minute it feels very light. If I hold it for an hour, I'll have an ache in my arm. If I hold it for a whole day, my arm will feel numb and paralysed. Any longer than that and I will be very tempted to give up and drop it. In each case, the weight of the glass doesn't change, but the longer I hold it, the heavier it becomes.'

The students were all blown away by the simplicity yet truth of this lesson.

However, the professor continued, 'the stresses and worries in life are like this glass of water. Carry them for only a short while and they're manageable. Worry about them a bit longer and they begin to hurt. And if we think about them all day long, or longer, we can begin to feel paralysed and hopeless – incapable of concentrating or focusing on anything else'.

The professor reminded his students 'it's important to remember to let go of your stresses whenever possible. As early in the evening as you can, put all your burdens down. Don't carry them through the evening and into the night. This can certainly be easier said than done in some cases, but in many cases it's actually quite easy if we're mindful about it'.

Within each of these four key principles our motivation to achieve success vs. to avoid failure, plays a significant role. Each principle can be viewed from both sides of the continuum and therefore interpreted differently. Your role in this chapter is to consider the model and how you have responded to each of those principles dependent of the motivational mindset you are in. As a single example, consider an individual who is in the MTS mindset and is faced with a challenge in which discipline is required, the MTS mindset is likely to drive the individual to continue down their chosen path and feedback will be interpreted very differently than if the individual is MTAF.

RECRUITING TALENT

The goal of all organisations is to ensure you have employed the right people with the right mindset and ensure they are doing the right work. If only it was that easy. Considering the perspective of this book, I am not going to suggest how you recruit and manage your talent, but I will challenge you and ask you to question the methodology you apply. Recruiting companies by definition are external organisations tasked with finding individuals who meet a certain criteria to fill a role. While the organisation clearly has the final say in who is successful, there appears to me to be one missing perspective. Who didn't make the cut? Over the past decade you would have noticed an increase in the amount of new roles that simply didn't exist ten years ago. Some degrees, which were completed in the 90's, don't even exist today and yet those individuals have still found a place in our economy. Positions that are currently being advertised don't even have a degree associated with them. This leaves an interesting challenge for recruiters as they have aligned individuals to roles. The added complexity is that they also need to align the individuals to the culture of the organisation. This is where it becomes interesting. I challenge anyone out there to try to quantify and explain the culture of his or her organisation! Let's be honest, it is simply not possible! We attempt to explain what it is like to work somewhere and define some of the acceptable behaviours but this only comes close to explaining a culture. The issue we face is that within every organisation there are a number of climates which are best described by the individuals who work in that specific area. The climates within an organisation are often described in greater and more specific detail than the overall culture. Consider when a friend from another country asks what the weather is like where you live? Your answer will always be relevant to which part of the country are you referring to. Companies are exactly the same, so unless the recruiter spends a significant amount of time in the department the applicant will be working in, they will struggle to recruit.

So how do you ensure you have the right person? Without giving too much away this early, I encourage you to read Greg Braddy's chapter (see page 93) and pay specific attention to his thoughts on building a team. The overall goal here is to ensure you have a solid diverse perspective. While specific experience is important, as are degrees, some of the most talented people possess neither of these. The process of recruiting is a difficult one and it has been well documented that to replace an individual will cost a business about 150 per cent of the total salary of the role. Especially when you take into account that a new recruit will determine if they are going to stay in a role within the first 30 days – but will take up to 18 months to actually move on. One can only wonder how productive they actually are, assuming they had decided to leave in the first 30 days. Additionally, we know people will stay in a role they dislike longer if they like the people they are working with, rather than if they like the role but dislike their co-workers. So it's worth spending the time to get it right.

TALENT MANAGEMENT

Managing talent once it is in your business can be as challenging as finding the right people in the right roles. For individuals to be successful they not only have to contribute to the outcome of the organisation but they also need to support the climate and ultimately make their teammates better. It is this last point that I want to focus on in this section. I accept that individuals who are skilled and exceptional at their job should be promoted but I would like to suggest that you add an extra element to your consideration. Do they make others around them better? Several years ago I interviewed Lindsay Gaze (retired Australian Olympic Basketball and Melbourne Tigers Coach) and while we discussed a number of aspects of high performance, the most interesting insight he shared was about a player who had attempted to secure a NBA contract on several occasions. He was an incredibly talented player, had won numerous individual accolades for his performances but he lacked a specific skill. After his last unsuccessful attempt to secure a contract, Lindsay spoke to the NBA recruiting manager wanting to understand why. The feedback was poignant. 'He has amazing skills, in fact I witnessed him dunk the ball on one of our superstars. His ability to shoot is second to none and his speed is fantastic. The problem is he doesn't know how to make his teammates look better. We already have a number of athletes who are incredibly skilled and one more will not necessarily make much of a difference. What we need is someone who can use their skills and support the team.' I think this insight is incredibly useful when considering your talent management program. Individuals need to have the right mindset to go along with their skills and experience. This mindset should primarily be focused on the process of making others better. The ultimate goal of any leader is to develop a high performing team and this usually means they have to let go of being 'the best' in the team. The motivational mindset plays a significant role here – consider the leader who becomes motivated to avoid failure in an attempt to protect their role – it simply can't work. The most successful leaders have found a way to ensure they remain motivated to succeed and create a climate around them that allows their teams to follow suit.

The basketball player in mention was motivated to avoid failure and therefore continually needed to prove how great he was. The concept of making others better came with a potential for perceived failure (He may not have scored as many points as he would have liked), so he chose not to take that path! 'Know, accept and perform your role.' Key things that people do that act as an inhibitor to their success is they try to lead by doing, not by leading. You need to accept that your role is to let others do what they need to do for the team to be successful.

Keep reading to gain some individual insights into how leaders achieve this.

Part II

This portion of the book is a series of interviews with senior executives who lead businesses located in Australia and around the world. The goal of this section is to provide you with a plethora of ideas that you can steal with pride. I use those words specifically as we all recognise that we don't have to reinvent the wheel but we should also acknowledge where we obtained the idea. Your job therefore is to integrate it into your own world and own it. You can never be like the people in this part of the book but you can always strive to be a better version of yourself! Remember nobody actually knows what they are doing when they go into a new role. Everybody makes it up as they go. You only go into a new role to get stretch. You don't typically move into a role if you already know how to do everything, as that's not challenging.

Before we start I would like to share a snippet from an interview conducted for my first book, *The Business Olympian* with an incredibly successful CEO, who due to the nature of his business has chosen to remain anonymous. The story he shared was extremely profound and provides a wonderful example of the motivational mindset in action.

The HR Director and the CFO – opposite motivations

Sitting in what would be one of the most inviting offices, the CEO was commenting on the drive of his board. I asked what he thought motivated them. He replied that they were all very different and driven by a variety of stimuli. Before he could continue with his explanation, I interrupted him and began discussing the concepts of motivation to succeed and motivation to avoid failure. At the end of my monologue, he sat back in his chair, thought for a while and said:

You have just perfectly described both my Human Resources Director and my Chief Finance Officer. That would have to be the most succinct way of understanding their behaviours I have ever heard. My HR Director has never met a challenge she didn't throw herself into. She is driven by achieving, what you referred to as success – she calls it her mission in life. Her failures are met with a sense of learning, she usually spends some time evaluating what went wrong and then heads right back out there to have another shot at it. My CFO is the complete opposite. He is very cautious and absolutely hates it when I go into his office to challenge something or query a line in the monthly profit and loss statement.His department is the most conservative department in the business. I can't remember the last time a sense of innovation made its way out of his office. Don't get me wrong, this is a billion dollar business, so he is doing a phenomenal job but I guess using your theory I wonder where we would be if there was a different motivation driving him.

GIAM SWIEGERS
CEO – Aurecon, formerly Deloitte

Giam Swiegers is a well-travelled CEO who has managed to conquer the commercial world on two continents and in two languages. As a native South African, he started his career with Deloitte South Africa and worked in both South Africa and the United States before immigrating to Australia in 1997. By 2000 he had been promoted to COO. In 2003 he was again promoted, this time to CEO where he undertook one of the largest transformational change programs the company had ever experienced. He retired as CEO in 2015, leaving behind a legacy of "Mr Fix it" as described by Business Review Weekly (BRW). He also left Deloitte in the best commercial position of its history, with over 640 partners and 6,500 staff members. In 2012/13 Deloitte turned over a billion dollars in revenue for the first time. Giam has been well known for promoting diversity in the workforce and has been a strong supporter of equal opportunity. In 2005 he was awarded the Best CEO for the advancement of women in business by the Equal Opportunity for Women in the Workplace Board, (an Australian Government Department), and in 2006 Giam was recognised by the Australian HR Awards, winning the 'HR Champion – CEO' award. Giam was a Founding Member of the Sex Discrimination Commissioner's Male Champions of Change Group. He sits on the UNSW's Australian School of Business Advisory Council and in February 2015 Giam accepted the role as Global CEO for Aurecon, a position he currently holds.

When I started to write this chapter, Giam was already preparing for his retirement from the role he had held for almost 12 years. He made time to speak with me, as I was keen to include some of his perspectives and philosophies, and to capture some examples from his experience in the journey he had been through with Deloitte. An imposing man, standing well over 6 feet tall, he speaks with an aura of authority and an undertone of humility and passion for the work he does and the people he works with. Having worked for Giam for a short period of time, I have experienced numerous interactions, which would never make the media reports but will always stand out for me as moments that mattered. I share with you my first interaction with him, to give you a sense of the man you don't see in the articles or the boardroom. I joined Deloitte Australia as a lateral hire director a number of years ago, with the hope of enhancing my commercial acumen and supporting the business in a new offer of leadership it was developing. As a lateral hire, I wasn't overtly aware of some of the cultural undertones in a large partnership (having never worked in one before) and the protocols in place for contacting and interacting with the senior leadership. Staying aligned to my own personal values, I decided to email Giam in his role as the CEO, introduce myself and invite him to join me for a cup of coffee. After hitting the send button, I must admit I didn't think I would get a positive response to the coffee invite and I had set a 4–6 week expectation of a response to my email. Within 12 hours not only did he respond with a welcoming email, but I also received a call from Michele his EA (an amazing person whose attention to detail and ability to see all of Giam's moving pieces and align them perfectly, is second to none) and had a coffee date set on his next trip to Melbourne where I was based. The most fascinating aspect of this interaction was when I shared my story with a local partner who had worked his way up in the organisation from a graduate to partner. His response was both amazing and astonishing. He said that the only time he had ever spoken to Giam was when they promoted him to partner, and he has never asked for a meeting since nor was he planning to. I always wondered why this individual responded in that manner; when relaying this story to Giam and asking him to define the type of people he works with, his response was fascinating.

The people who join the big four firms are generally highly intelligent, highly ambitious and highly insecure.

To back up this statement he added, 'we used to have significant amounts of data on this and through the use of psychometric testing determined that about 80 per cent of partner's rate highly on the insecurity factor'. Giam's hypothesis was that insecure people tended to study subjects that have predictive outcomes, 'engineering, law and accounting were favoured by those with higher levels of insecurity while more secure people favoured marketing, advertising and psychology'. He admits that the research project was never completed but maintains that the data was overtly convincing. If you consider the big four accounting firms, you will notice that they all have a very predictive base with auditing and accounting forming the main pillars. It was only later on that the consulting side emerged and even then, the departments of human capital and leadership were the last to join. One could argue that human beings have the least amount of predictability and as they say, 'never bet on a game where the ball wasn't round and the opposition was unpredictable'. Conversely, accounting and even technology consulting have a significantly higher level of predictability built into them.

On the motivational continuum, Giam recognises that some of his staff comfortably fit into the motivation to avoid failure (MTAF) mindset, as the high need for success, coupled with a significant fear of failure, ultimately creates an individual who can thrive in this type of environment. So how do you motivate a large group of people in this mindset and subtly try to guide them away from 'fear of failure' as the motivator and into success as the motivator? Giam refers to the As One theory, which was developed by his team in conjunction with other global Deloitte based teams, 'We needed to provide them with an incredibly strong WHY. They had to understand exactly not just what we wanted them to do but a well-constructed and deeply passionate WHY. When I started, my goal for the first 6 years was to be the most inspirational place to work'. This was a lofty goal given the position Deloitte was in the early 2000's. He could not hide behind this theory, as Deloitte's position in the market was well known. 'I wanted people who were joining us to know we may be the weakest of the big four but we were the most aspirational and willing to grow and change'. He was also very clear that if his staff did not have the courage to fight against the better brands, even when the likelihood of success was low, then, 'You were just not right for this organisation'.

I once saw a definition of courage, which I still use to this day.

Courage is the commitment to begin without any guarantee of success.

Giam explained, 'Once we had them on board, we just needed to make the case for 'why' it is possible. Part of that was why we were different and why we chose to enter into sections of the market where others chose not to'. He stressed that his part in the process was recognising the intellectual capital of his team and making the point, 'going where no other firms chose to go, actually provided us with a platform to make our mark, define who we were and realistically there was also going to be less resistance'. He argued that going head to head with other firms in areas in which they were 'simply better than us' just did not make sense. Motivation in this circumstance could never have worked. He had no evidence that his approach would work, nor did he have a crystal ball, which could have predicted the outcome. What he did have was an inspirational message, which started at the core of the new Deloitte. 'It would have been too hard to try and motivate each person; we needed an overriding inspirational message which could then be owned by the individual, allowing them to motivate themselves.' Giam, by both insight and circumstance, came to the commercial apex and made a choice which had his people squarely at the centre of his decision making process.

But do leaders always get it right?

One could question how an organisation could ever get into this kind of state, a set of values come to mind and are printed below.

VALUES
Respect – *We treat others as we would like to be treated ourselves. We do not tolerate abusive or disrespectful treatment. Ruthlessness, callousness and arrogance don't belong here.*
Integrity – *We work with customers and prospects openly, honestly, and sincerely. When we say we will do something,*

*we will do it; when we say we cannot or will not do
something, then we won't do it.*

Communication *– We have an obligation to communicate.
Here, we take the time to talk with one another and to
listen. We believe that information is meant to move and
that information moves people.*

Excellence *– We are satisfied with nothing less than the
very best in everything we do. We will continue to raise the
bar for everyone. The great fun here will be for all of us to
discover just how good we can really be.*

On the surface this looks like a great set of words and to be honest the
word-smithing of the descriptors is second to none. The fundamental
problem with this set of values is that they belong to an organisation
called Enron, who in 2001 declared bankruptcy. At that time they
employed about 20,000 people and it was one of the world's major
electricity, natural gas, communications and pulp and paper companies.
In 2000 they declared revenue of nearly USD$111 billion, only one
year later the company didn't exist. The reason for the collapse has
been identified as an institutionalised systematic and creatively planned
accounting fraud, perpetuated by its senior executive team. Leaders who
cannot live their own values and who through violate their values with
their actions, create an environment in which individuals become highly
motivated to avoid failure.

Giam reflected on when he had seen leaders fail to live up to the
values they had promised to keep. 'I recall a leader who wholeheartedly
believed in "spin", he believed it was vital to keep people believing in
the rhetoric regardless of what was actually happening around them;
he would deliberately put a positive spin on all information especially
negative information'. The problem with this approach from Giam's

perspective is that 'insecure, smart people will see straight through it immediately, and once they believe you are lying to them, your ability to inspire is lost forever, as is trust'. He has described perfectly a concept called the confirmation bias, in which your preconceived perception of a person is continually reinforced, by even the smallest of corresponding behaviours. 'People would always look for the lie in everything they said'. How can you expect to lead and inspire an organisation if you have lost trust? You may have power, which is granted through your position, but trust is an emotion and felt through your emotional brain – if we return to chapter one, the flow on the effect of losing trust should be obvious.

Prior to taking on the CEO role, Giam recalled a number of moments in which the previous Deloitte leadership chose to use spin rather than the truth. 'It was the toughest time in my career', he said. During this time, he came to the conclusion that he could not continue in his current role and decided to leave the firm. During his notice period the Board ultimately decided to remove the incumbent and offered the CEO role to Giam. History tells us that he made the right decision to accept the position. He recalled the first partnership workshop he held, in which he laid out his view of the world and in particular his view of the Deloitte world. 'It was the harshest meeting I think this partnership had ever experienced', but the most consistent feedback he received was 'at last we have heard the truth'. More importantly, he informed me they 'believed that someone is going to try and fix it, because we called it as it is'.

Fast forward 12 years and just prior to him leaving Deloitte, he had well over 6,500 employees and over 640 partners. Deloitte had moved from the smallest of the big four, (described by the press in 2003 as a "sick puppy") to clearly the second largest firm. It was for all intent and purposes a very different commercial business from the one he inherited

12 years earlier. Does the same philosophy apply now to a large team? How do you inspire a large organisation, dispersed in geography and distanced from the executive team? Giam maintains that while 'you can't touch each person individually, you can ensure the consistency in your communication as well as its regularity'. He further added 'each message needs to be a well-made argument. The document should be an argument to your team that this road will produce a better outcome, don't always just rely on your managers to spread your word. You as a leader need to let them hear it from you as much as possible'. Modern technology has created an environment in which no leader can be excused from not communicating with their team on a regular basis. Deloitte has always prided themselves in the adoption of new technology and Giam was one of the first CEOs to actively use Yammer to not only spread his message but also as a tool in which his team could reply. Although he does worry that 'people are so connected nowadays that they almost become unconnected', I think what he was referring to was the numbing sensation we experience when we are subjected to too many stimuli. His research suggested to him that about 25 per cent of the firm used emails; 20 per cent read DAIS (their online platform); a reasonable number of people followed Yammer (an online corporate version of Twitter) and some watched videos depending on who was sending the message. Giam's approach was to use all channels, assuming he would reach about 70 per cent of his team. Which still meant 30 per cent were left not hearing his message, in which case he hoped that they would find out what he was saying from someone else as a result of its consistent repetition across all channels. One very important factor to consider with communication is that your most preferred form is likely driven by a series of unconscious biases. That means you will assume people will simply get your message. You will find it incredibly difficult to focus on other forms, due to the discomfort, but this will ultimately allow

you to recraft the message and hopefully ensure the full intent is being conveyed.

On the most recent partner survey, before his retirement, Giam was very proud to report that on several of the most important elements of the business argument; over 90 per cent of the partners were in agreement. It really makes an individual's life easier when your senior leaders are on song with your plan. He commented, 'The question I still ask them is, it's great that you are in agreement with the plan, but what are you going to do to support the pathways to success'. He was by default shifting the accountability of success to the individuals and allowing them to determine the best pathway forward for themselves. The process of allowing individuals to be accountable for their own success and therefore also accountable for their own failures is paramount in fostering a high performing environment and a team motivated to succeed.

Giam recognised that even though his leadership style may not have been very accommodating early on in his career, he still realised that you needed to 'create the argument and then allow individuals to determine how they will succeed within those parameters, you were on to a formula for success'. He gave a simple yet elegant example.

> *Let's consider a new receptionist is starting, you could go to them with a list of 'things' to do, I want you to smile, I want you to get visitors a glass of water etc. All they have is a checklist and they will determine they have done a good job if all items have been checked on the list, but will they really do it, who knows? Or you say 'you are the director of first impressions, we need our clients to have a great experience, work out what that means for each and every client and make it happen'.*

The Deloitte front line team does not have a job description, there are no checklists or guidelines, and they are not executing against a set of expectations and so are truly allowed to create the best possible greeting for each and every client. Giam explained, 'when you walk into the office, there are no desks, our staff walk around and are free to support our guests in the best way they see fit. You can't help but reflect that this is different, and hopefully this translated through the rest of the Deloitte experience'. He did accept that even with the best of intentions, Sydney has been the only office he has been able to convert to the no reception desk policy. 'I tried with the others, but I guess they wanted to do it their way. Each reception staff member plays the important role – in their own way – of making every client feel special'. Under Giam's steerage, this would still be OK.

But does fear still play a role? 'Fear will always be there but I am very conscious that it paralyses very, very quickly and stops people from doing things. The bigger issue is that it creates a culture where people will simply wait for instructions.' This however needs to be finely balanced with the concepts of consequence management. Giam continued, 'if you don't have consequences for the wrong behaviour, they will never change'. It is important to recognise that cultures are created through conversations; people will talk and share their experiences as well as their interpretations of events. If an individual is allowed to behave in a certain manner, which is deemed inappropriate by their peers, and management chooses to ignore it, it sends a very strong message about the culture of the organisation and ultimately impacts on the motivational mindset. Giam reflected on how much fear is required to manage behaviour and commented, 'you need some fear but how much and where is the line between fear and respect? I don't know – I have never been able to work that out'. The fundamental reason why Giam was unable to work it out is because of the motivational mindset, which can be explained perfectly using Ben Johnson, the disgraced athlete as an example.

If during the 1988 Seoul Olympics, especially at the conclusion of the 100m sprint, I had asked you to consider Ben Johnson and comment on the type of athlete you thought he was, I am confident that the majority of people would have deemed him to be on the 'Motivation to Succeed' side of the continuum. He had overcome the 10 second barrier and set a new Olympic and world record for the 100 meter sprint of 9.79 seconds. Realistically, at this point he was sitting on top of the sprinting world. However, within hours of being the golden athlete of the games, he became a pariah and was labelled a cheat. He had failed his drug test and his medal was stripped from him. His world was about to come crashing down; he had his previously won titles taken from him, endorsements were going fast and the public started to see him for who he really was, an individual who was so motivated to avoid failure that he demonstrated almost every single attribute I described in chapter two (if only Lance Armstrong had learned from this example). The problem we face as leaders is that we simply cannot know what people are thinking and what their motivations are until they overtly present themselves. Giam's inability to determine where the line is not a reflection on his leadership skills. It is actually indicative of his humanity and the fact that we cannot read minds, and at best have to rely on fuzzy indicators, and dare I say, gut feelings. In spite of this, Giam is very clear that 'people should realise that if they get paid to do a job and they don't live up to the norms that are set, that income will be taken away from them. I believe and sincerely hope that we did a good job of removing individuals, not who were fearful of failure, but who were willing to cheat'. For Giam, this included individuals who were very senior and some part of the original executive team in the late 90's who had created the issue of spin discussed earlier. Up until a couple of years prior to his departure, Giam interviewed every single senior lateral hire partner the firm was looking to recruit. 'I wanted to know that they could deal with a weak brand that wanted to fight back, and I wanted to look them in the eye and make sure they were on the same page as everyone else – we needed to be street fighters and work incredibly hard to make up the ground we had lost'. He simply could not have individuals who were not prepared to work as a team. He needed them to be inspired by the thought that they could actually make a difference, build something and have their fingerprints all over the success, 'The psychology of a consulting firm is paramount, it's like a sporting team, when it's on it's on, but when its off, it really is off'. As a small side note, over the ten years that followed the 1988 Seoul Olympic Games almost every other athlete in that 100m sprint tested positive to a banned substance, including the great Carl Lewis (although his was for an inadvertent use of pseudoephedrine).

Giam was also very cognisant of the fact that Deloitte was moving through a phase where cost cutting was a focal point and felt that 'the people who were in charge of the cost cutting gained far greater control of the firm than they should have'. On the topic of the downside of this outcome, Giam said 'the messaging became negative and I believe some may have interpreted that as failing. We actually went into February 2014 with a doom and gloom attitude – incredible for a billion dollar organisation. We were missing revenue targets by around 2.5 per cent. 2.5 per cent on a billion dollar revenue target and we managed to make the firm feel like losers'. Giam changed the messaging, completely revamped the style and content of the communication and put forward a case that 'we are the momentum firm, why would we get depressed on an outcome which given the economic times was actually remarkable and we switched on a little button and it only took till June for the craziness to return. While there were a number of activities which occurred, the most prominent was the change in tone'. It is incredible to note how powerful a motivational and inspirational message can be, but more importantly how quickly you can change direction in a large organisation. 'We were ignited' reflected Giam, clearly a man who was still deeply passionate about his organisation and the legacy he wanted to leave behind. 'I wanted them to know they hadn't let us down, in fact we were greatly appreciative of how well we were succeeding – June 2014 was the month of records, all time record revenue, billings and every other measure of financial success'. This was in spite of the economy maintaining its status quo.

As his time with Deloitte was soon to come to a natural conclusion, the organisation and the market were aware of his impending departure and the internal mechanism for appointing his replacement was well under way. With that process in mind, what should be the focus for the next CEO – what could phase two look like? Being the underdog and hunting the larger brands is often seen to be easier as you have less to lose, but what about when the tables are turned? Giam's advice to the next CEO was insightful.

> *The next CEO is going to have a number of challenges but the greatest one in my mind is to ensure that we maintain our hunger and recognise how we arrived in this situation yet ensure we have a solid goal to focus the future on. Many new recruits would not understand the past and would not have that platform to drive their motivation, while those who joined the underdog may now be reflecting on the current position and recognising we are no longer the underdog.*

A couple of years earlier, two of Giam's major teams challenged his interpretation of their position in the market, suggesting that in fact they were actually number one and requested he stop referring to Deloitte as number two or three. 'I disagreed with them and continued to watch their performance. Two years later both those teams failed this organisation, because the two leaders never understood the psychological impact it was going to have on the teams when they played that card. People started thinking we chased it and we are now there so 'what now?' Giam still firmly believes that if those two leaders had maintained the overall team perception the firm would be in an even better situation. With Deloitte's current position in the market, one can only speculate as to how Deliotte's new CEO will overcome the 'what now?' challenge.

TAKE HOME

» It can be easy to be hungry and drive a team, but much harder when you achieve your goals and then have to push further. Always reset your goals to keep you ahead of the pack.

» Talent is important, but fit is paramount.

» What you say and what you do must be congruent.

» Define your business plan as an argument and then convince everyone else.

» Use all forms of communication – leave your favourite to last as it can be driven by a bias.

» Selling doom and gloom as a threat to motivation, is counter-productive and likely to cause stress and anxiety. Honesty and transparency is the only option.

DARYL JOHNSON
CEO – NAB Asia

Daryl Johnson has over 35 years banking experience internationally. His most recent role was CEO Asia for National Australia Bank (NAB), based in Singapore. Daryl's prior role with NAB was Executive General Manager NAB Business. In this position he was responsible for leading more than 2,500 small and medium enterprises (SME) bank relationship managers across Australia. Prior to this, he led NAB's Corporate Banking business in Australia.

Before joining NAB, Daryl held senior executive roles within ANZ, spanning Business, Corporate and Retail Banking both in Australia and Asia. Roles at ANZ included: Managing Director Business Banking, Senior General Manager Auto Finance, General Manager Merchant Services and Chief Operating Officer Business Banking. He has extensive experience in all areas of banking, in particular corporate and commercial markets. He has also led large-scale transformations within the businesses he has overseen.

Daryl holds a Master of Business Administration from Murdoch University in Western Australia and a Bachelor of Business (Financial Management and Economics) from Curtin University in Western Australia. He is also a Graduate of the Australian Institute of Company Directors and has served on the board of youth charity organisations, Whitelion and Open Family Australia. He is a keen cyclist and golfer and is currently in France undertaking an intensive French language program.

My first meeting with Daryl is one I will never forget. After a meeting with his HR business partner we needed to get Daryl's final sign off on an executive workshop I was proposing. It was a two-

81

day workshop with the overall goal of gaining alignment within his team on the upcoming change program sweeping through NAB. The outcome of the program was a systematic change in the way his several thousand employees worked. It was very apparent that while his immediate leadership team was on board, this level of support was not as forthcoming from the senior management team below. I was tasked with taking the team on a journey of not just change but understanding the psychology of working in a completely new and foreign format.

Daryl is a man who is completely comfortable in his own space and had delegated the design of this workshop to his team, so on the surface this was going to be a tick and flick exercise; except for the morning of day two. Here is where it got very interesting. In my design, I deliberately selected an activity that was going to make his team feel completely out of their comfort zone and challenge them to the very core of their rhetoric around being adaptable to change. The day was going to start with his team learning a hip hop dance routine and proving that NAB employees do think they can dance. This was then followed up by a trip to a basketball court and the challenge of learning an offence routine and demonstrating that routine under pressure. (The pressure being that I was recording their effort and they were being watched by a small group of bystanders). After presenting my idea the room became very quiet and Daryl just looked at me. His initial response was as expected, 'there is no way I am dancing' but as fast as he said it he caught his words, reflected on the task at hand and said, 'well if we can't challenge ourselves to do something out of our comfort zone, how can we ever ask our people to do the same'.

Daryl would be the first to agree that he would definitely never make it as a backup dancer but he gave it a red hot go. I think he secretly enjoyed it though I could never get him to admit it. After leading the rollout of the One-Way-Same-Way change transformation program, Daryl continued as General Manager of NAB Corporate before taking up a similar role with NAB Business and finally heading over to Singapore to lead the NAB Asia team as CEO.

It was during his time as CEO in Asia that we met again to explore the concept of motivation and how culture plays a role. His comment on that was, 'it's a very interesting situation in Asia because of the different cultures. We have an offices in Singapore, Hong Kong, China, Japan, India, Vietnam, and Indonesia and it's hugely different in terms of what people want, what their lives are about, and what they're motivated by'. Daryl provided some advice on how to handle these disparate cultural differences.

> *First, you need to try and understand the high level cultural differences around different countries, ethnicities and religions. An Australian doing business in Asia will encounter many cultural differences and it is critical that these differences are considered when communicating with your teams. However, it remains important to get back to the core of understanding the individuals, not just high-level cultural issues. What is it that drives this person? How do I build a personal connection with this person? One thing that remains the same across these different cultural settings and types of people is they all want personal rapport and understanding with the people they work with.*

NAB doesn't have a significant footprint in Asia and his team was small by his standards.

We have about 550 people in total. We have a matrix leadership structure, with the geographic leaders reporting directly to me. We then have another half a dozen people that run the global lines of business in Asia. These leaders have dual reporting lines to me and to others in the organisation. Combined these 12 people are our Asia leadership team.

Daryl spent a signification amount of time ensuring that this team work effectively across the various continents and lines of business.

Not withstanding the challenge of leading the senior team, Daryl actually described his greater challenge being how to 'connect through to a relatively junior person sitting in Japan or Mumbai'. It is often during times like this where you are being challenged in a different way that you pause and consider your core values and the style of leader you want to be, fortunately for Daryl he had a mentor early in his career who really helped focus his style.

Many years ago in my career I was offered a really good promotion to go and work in project and structured finance. I was attracted by the intellectual complexity of the work and by the potential to do well financially. I went and talked to a guy who had been an advisor of mine who actually operated in that area. I wanted his opinion on if it was a good idea to go and work there. I thought he would tell me it was. Instead, he actually told me to think long and hard before going down a more specialised path because in his view there was less ability to influence what others were doing, and contributions were generally individual or small team based. He told me that after having done his job for 25 years, talented young people that were coming up were the enemy rather than an asset. They were the enemy because they were all trying to get his job. This really stuck in my mind and I suddenly thought. How do you make more of a difference?

Creating alignment and consistency across the workforce is paramount to effective leadership.

Get an appropriate strategy in place and provide clarity of what you're trying to achieve. I think you can amplify the impact by having good leaders who have a consistent message, broadly consistent values, or at least values that you're happy with and can give a broader team a sense of purpose, a sense of meaning and also some guidance on what the key areas of focus should be. I see many people trying to focus on too many things. The reality is if they really focused on the two, three or five things that mattered most to their role, they would probably be more successful. Leaders have the responsibility to help people achieve the right focus.

To Daryl, motivating and leading is all about leverage. 'The trick is to get your leadership group on the same page and to make sure that they are as aligned as possible. Ensure that when they are going and talking to the teams, they actually have a consistent story'. Another important form of alignment in organisations is 'between what we say we want people to do and what we actually reward them for doing', which Daryl believes 'can often be quite different things'.

Managing and leading staff through a remuneration and benefits scheme is ultimately fraught with danger as for the most part they have to be designed to fit the lowest common denominator. I am not suggesting the schemes are designed for poor performers, but they are usually designed to meet the needs of the many, the exceptional and for that matter the unexceptional are often difficult to account for.

> *I'm not sure that I see too many organisations do it really well. I think young people – and of course everyone is different – want money and satisfaction in their job. They want to work with good people and feel they are making a difference and a contribution. If you're at the start of your career and you're ambitious, then career prospects and future opportunities could matter a lot. If you're in the latter stages of your career, maybe things have changed. Some people are deeply money driven. Others are not so focused on money. Maybe they've reached the point in their seniority where they're not ambitious anymore so future career path may not matter as much for them.*

Within a large and diverse organisation that has employees with different ages, experiences, and ambitions, Daryl highlights the importance of understanding each individual person.

> *I think it's a matter of working out what it is they want. Speaking personally, whilst I like money, I'm not as money focused as I used to be. I'm ambitious, but I'm not as ambitious as I used to be. I've probably got a lower tolerance to put up with working with people I don't regard, or spending my time on things that I don't really*

believe in because I want my job in the short term to be more fulfilling and satisfying. When I was 30 years old, I was probably willing to put up with a bit more of short term pain in exchange for this option for the future and so on.

The ability to motivate a team is often seen as a reflection of the tools provided for by the organisation. Leaders will often defer to the system or the lack of certain processes as to the reasons for their inability to gain the best performance out of their people. Daryl shared a practical challenge he had faced with a worker who as a result of being 'very senior, hugely capable, with plenty of options and well off financially' was very difficult to motivate. This worker in particular was trying to work through whether NAB was the place for him to stay for the short, medium and long term.

Strategy will be what it is, the culture will be what it is, and there is a lot of good about that, but there is a fit issue. So my questions to him have been: Why is it you want this job? Why do you come to work every day? What is it you want from your work? I can't tell him he should work here. The discussion I want to have with him is, what is important in his work life at this point in time, and then, how strong is the alignment that we have at this organisation? If they are close and if he can get satisfaction out of it, I'm saying to him that he should stay, but he needs to stop being negative about some of the things he's allowing to annoy him. I've also said that if there are too many negatives, why are you staying? Why would you work here? He's at a stage in his life where he's quite difficult to please. Which is great for him because he's got so many freedoms.

This interaction captures the essence of this book's title perfectly. There is no real point in trying to motivate this individual. The tools at Daryl's discretion were as useful as using a flat head screwdriver to unscrew a Philips head screw, there is a chance you could do it, but it's going to take forever and you need to have the exact right size to fit the groove. You will notice that Daryl very early on in the piece recognised that traditional methods of motivation were simply not going to work and he instead started a conversation with an inspirational undertone. He turned the message around and challenged the individual to find the motivation within but to be sure this was the best place for him. He did however set the guidelines, indicating that if he chose to stay then there were some parameters that were non-negotiable. Getting an individual to be accountable for their actions is paramount. Daryl concluded by saying: 'I have to approach my interactions with this person with a high degree of directness and honesty because I don't want him wasting his time and I don't want him becoming a disgruntled senior person and not be productive to the organisation if there's not going to be a good fit'.

But sometimes you can have a more direct approach. 'A guy ten years younger who was ambitious and really needed the money, would be much easier to motivate. Although I would still want them to work for me for the right reasons, because money as an incentive to work loses its value the minute it hits your pocket'. Daryl extrapolates this idea of fit in an organisation, to a talent program that NAB has launched, which does not aim to 'measure one month, or six months later the benefit that NAB has gotten out of it', but instead is 'an investment in the individual', and allows for a personal assessment of fit to the organisation.

It is actually about helping them understand themselves better, working through what it is that's important in their life, the events in their life that have influenced them and shaped them to be what they are, what they are trying to achieve in life and how work and career fits within that. We've had people go through that program and focus on things that have got nothing to do with work. Focus on improving their relationship with a parent, getting fit, or investing more in their marriage.

To be truly an inspirational leader you need to put the person at the centre of your diagram, with the return on investment to the organisation being a variable which they can impact on, not the other way round. This position can be very confronting especially when good people decide to leave and choose another pathway because you may have been counting on them to achieve a specific goal and this decision is going to impact on that. However, the effect on that person staying in the wrong environment has far greater ramifications.

At the time of our interview, Daryl was in the process of launching this talent program in Asia in a slightly different format to the one in the Australian launch and gave further insight.

We're just launching that (the talent program) in Asia to appeal to members of the team who are at earlier stages of their career and are probably still trying to work out how this career fits into the rest of their life, whether they are happy being here or not and why they are working for a foreign bank in Asia. In some ways I don't care what decisions they ultimately come to. We might lose some good people (that's not the desire of course) because they decide that working for a big company like NAB doesn't make sense. My view is that if they actually come to that view sooner rather than sitting here being unhappy for five years, that's probably a good outcome. For others, they might feel that they were unsure about working for us, but they might see this investment in them as what it is, as a genuine investment and it could be something that makes them feel more positive about the organisation.

During his time at NAB Daryl completed a number of personal development programs and one in particular resonated with him. The outcome of this program was the development of his own personal leadership point of view. It is a very personal document and he has agreed to share some components of it. This section has been unedited and is presented in the format I received it.

Leadership brings with it privileges and obligations that makes being a leader a very rewarding experience. For me, the greatest privilege of leadership is the opportunity to deliver value through a team that significantly exceeds the value that I could deliver individually. Satisfying the obligations of leadership is in fact also enormously rewarding and in many ways, these obligations can also be seen as privileges. The key leadership obligation is to create an environment that provides every member of the team with the greatest possible opportunity to perform and grow both personally and professionally.

My personal values strongly influence my approach to; life in general, leadership and more broadly to business: they include: Trust, Honesty, Integrity, Loyalty,

Authenticity and Openness, Achievement, Enjoyment and Family.

In business, I am focused on the ultimate aim of assisting my organisation being the best in its field. From a personal perspective, I strive to make a difference to the business and I am highly committed to the delivery of results and to driving constructive change.

Having a clear strategic agenda is an important base for business success, but strategic plans should not be static and must adapt to changing conditions. Key components of a successful business strategy will include a strong external focus on customers and an internal focus on collaboration and action. Smart leaders will drive strategic execution, but will also be open minded to opportunistic moves.

Having the best people in key leadership roles is a key driver of business success as leaders are the leverage points for business outcomes. The performance of any given team will be influenced highly by the quality of their leader.

Business is about winning. Combining strategic clarity, high quality leaders and a collaborative, action focused environment will dramatically increase business success

My leadership approach is inclusive and I work hard to engage my teams. I am known as frank, decisive and genuine. I provide strategic clarity and ensure that the team have significant autonomy in running their businesses. This autonomy comes with responsibility, accountability and significant recognition for those who succeed. I work actively to better enable people to succeed in their roles and to grow as people, both professionally and personally.

My leadership style is informal and I build close relationships with others, irrespective of our style differences. My results focus is countered with a strong desire for the team to share in success and have fun, even when the going is tough.

I would encourage you to ask yourself: What is your leadership point of view? Why should anyone be led by you? On completion you will find the underpinning of any motivational/leadership conversation you will ever have. Your next challenge is determining how you will share this?

TAKE HOME

» Every message will have two interpretations, the one meant and the one understood. They may be different!

» Use a mentor and seek advice from people who are not emotionally invested in your career.

» Amplify the message through your people.

» When driving a strategy work hard to get everyone on the same page.

» Be conscious of what we ask people to do and what we actually reward them for doing.

» Employees and organisations both need to understand the why:

  » Why we exist,

  » Why I want to work here.

» Beating around the bush simply wastes time and doesn't help your authenticity. Be honest and talk it through.

» Talent development should begin before they know they are talent.

GREG BRADDY
Executive General Manager, Chief Financial Officer – NAB Business Bank

Greg commenced his career with PricewaterhouseCoopers (then Coopers and Lybrand) Melbourne in January 1988. During his career with PwC, Greg provided internal and external audit services to clients in Australia, Asia and the United Kingdom, with a specialisation in insurance and investment management.

Greg is a qualified Chartered Accountant and a member of the Institute of Internal Auditors. Greg was admitted to the partnership of PwC on 1 July 1999, a position he held until January 2007 when he joined National Australia Bank (NAB) as the Chief Financial Officer for NAB's Australian businesses. After two years as CFO, Greg was appointed as a Program Executive in NextGen and was subsequently appointed as Executive General Manager Audit for the NAB Group in October 2011.

As the chief internal auditor his role is to support the business by monitoring and testing the internal governance of all its systems and processes. He interacts regularly with the Chair of the Board Audit Committee. As this book was going to print, Greg received another promotion within the NAB group to Executive General Manager, Chief Financial Officer – Business Banking.

Like most people, Greg starts his day with the drive into work, but this is where the similarities possibly end. Most of us smile when we find a parking spot close to the lifts and then usually head on up, stopping maybe for a coffee on the way through. Greg starts his day a little differently by asking himself how he is feeling and what type of leadership mindset and mood state he is bringing into the workplace on that day. While somewhat unique, it is actually quite insightful and a surprisingly very powerful strategy we could all employ. The anecdotal theory of our mindset is that it is very much in flex that is we are able to alter our emotional mindset with a degree of ease. It is also very much dependent on the context of the situation we find ourselves in. Ever woken up on the wrong side of the bed – figuratively not literally? The concept of changing ones mindset or mood state is often debated and I give you this perspective for your consideration.

Take a moment and head off to find someone in your organisation and ask them with a degree of concern on your face, if everything was alright. I will bet that 99 per cent of people will look up, smile and say "yes, why?" and maybe continue by giving you some more insight into what they are doing or what deadline they are trying to meet. The interesting aspect here is that the smile is not a conscious reaction; it is the brain trying to demonstrate a sense of congruency. What do I mean by congruency in this sense? Very simply put the brain will attempt at all stages of consciousness to maintain a balance between our thoughts and our behaviour – it (the brain) likes to be congruent, what we feel is demonstrated in how we act. So when you point out to someone that they appear to be something that they are not (e.g sad) – the brain will go into overdrive and over-represent itself (the smile) to readjust the balance. There is a good chance the individual is not technically happy (which would explain the smile) but it is just one of those interesting phenomenon's which occurs.

This therefore suggests that we are able to change our mood states by first understanding our own feelings and secondly ensuring that we are checking in with ourselves on a regular basis to optimise the congruency. Greg's check-in in the parking lot gives him that opportunity to "smile" and readjust if he finds himself not quite where he wants to be. He admits, 'there are times for leadership reasons that I really need to turn on and that moment in the car really aids in that'. The natural question we would all ask at this point is how do I know when I am not quite where I want to be, what are the signs and symptoms I should look for? Greg has an interesting perspective suggesting, he starts with the evaluation of resilience and is cognisant of the requirements of his role and the impact it has emotionally. At the time of the interview he was reflecting that the last few weeks had been particularly challenging and therefore he was spending more time each morning focusing on exactly what was coming up that day and what specific energising actives he would require.

So where would you start? While Greg defines his "Car Check-in" as the essential part of the day, where is yours? And more importantly, once you have identified your current mood state, how would you change it if you need to. Over the years I have both experienced myself and heard from others some useful tips and tricks.

» Set a very specific goal that can be absolutely measured at the end of the day – very short term in nature and one, which will give you the sense of gratification regardless of the outcome. If the outcome is positive that's fantastic and if it is negative then you have tomorrow's goal already decided.

» Consider a break in your routine, have a walk around the building before you go in; buy someone a coffee and have a distracting conversation. Just don't do the same things you always do.

» Take a selfie (honestly I can't believe I actually wrote this, but the theory is sound – have a look at what you look like and then deliberately expand on the emotion. That is, if you are feeling crappy, put on the face and take a photo, and then decide if that is the face you want to take into the office.

» Check your diet. It's been known for years that different foods will affect our moods differently. If you don't believe me, give your kids or your neighbour's kids some sugar snakes for breakfast and sit back and watch the mayhem.

» Exercise, exercise and then exercise – but recognise the different types of exercise which are appropriate for your state of mind. If you are highly stressed then active exercise is not actually going to help. Once you are stressed you do not want to stress the body more so maybe relaxation or yoga is a better option. However, if you are simply feeling flat and have no energy then a brisk walk or run might be exactly what you need.

» Make a conscious decision to park some thoughts and put them aside so you can focus on what is required but always make the agreement to pick those thoughts back up and attend to them in due course.

Greg's secondary indicator after considering resilience is that he actually feels his stress in his stomach. 'It's a gut thing, I just seem to feel it there, but it is always associated to a thought process of, what are the implications of all of this, so I am continually aware of those indicators'. What Greg has courageously outlined here is that the behavioural angle is just as relevant as the cognitive one. We often ignore our behavioural symptoms and just assume they will go away or that we are weak for having them but I implore you to think about a work mate who has experienced burnout in the work place. The outcome is not pretty and there is usually no mechanism to stop it once it has happened. It occurs when we choose to ignore these symptoms. I am conscious here that burnout is in and of itself the topic of an entire book but it's not the focus of this book.

Here we are still in Greg's car, as usual he does not head into the building until the checks and balances are in place (being an auditor probably does help a little as well). Let's jump ahead and explore how this approach translates into his team and how he uses these insights to inspire his team.

Taking Audit to the Next Level

Greg has a large team who are charged with ensuring the systems and processes of the bank are being upheld to the highest possible standards and where appropriate make recommendations for improvement and sometimes even requests for alterations. To ensure his team members function at the highest level Greg spends an inordinate amount of time ensuring that they have, as he puts it, 'Great clarity around the vision of what we are trying to achieve'. He is the first to recognise that the statement of a "vision" may seem somewhat "motherly" but to him it is important that his team 'is fully aware of what we are trying to achieve and being very definitive about it'. His view is that if his team is very clear on what it is trying to achieve then 'we can engage people a lot more around how they can bring their best efforts to the process, which further allows us to celebrate the successes with our partners along the way'. Greg admits that he often uses sports psychology and the concept of sports motivation in his approach and recognises that the celebration of success is vital for both short but more importantly long term achievements. The great analogy with sport is that you won't always win the gold medal, but you can always strive to be better than your last effort and internalise the success.

At this stage, it all sounds wonderful and the roses are always in bloom, but even with all the best attempts there is always a chance that someone in the team just does not toe the line. Working with individuals who are not motivated can often be very challenging. Like the vast majority of senior executives, Greg over his many years in the corporate arena has come across individuals who in a sporting analogy were either, 'not up for the task' or 'riddled with significant self-doubt and negative talk' that were unable to perform to their potential. He describes these individuals as being 'the glass half empty sort of people, or focused on why something can't be done rather than what can be achieved – "the art of the possible"'. His approach to resolving these issues is to get on the front foot early, the longer you leave a person in this mindset, the more they believe in their own rhetoric, and before you know it the sporadic thoughts become consistent ones and the relevant behaviours become entrenched. By getting on the front foot Greg does two distinct things, which we can all learn from.

» He has the conversation as soon as possible and,
» He consciously prepares for it.

'I think long and hard about the coaching questions I am going to use and always very aware of my own authenticity, in making sure that I truly listen and understand their situation'. It is always important to remember that an individual will always have several aspects to their circumstances and Greg was very aware that their personal situation may also be at the root cause, 'I also need to create a safe environment for people to feel comfortable discussing their concern(s) with me, while at the same time allowing them to drive the conversation to the level they felt comfortable with'.

What Greg has so elegantly described is what psychologists have often referred to as a bi-directional expertise, which in a counselling environment, posits that the individual is the expert on their situation, while you, the psychologist have an expertise in models and other wonderful theories, all of which are useless unless the person sitting opposite you chooses to bring their expertise to the table.

Greg recalled a specific situation from several years ago that 'included a personal aspect which was affecting an individual, but through the conversation we were able to separate out the various factors and then explore the stressors which I could have some impact over'. Separating the various aspects of the individual's life, which are controllable in the work place, while at the same time recognising the impact of the personal issue, will provide an incredibly safe and comfortable environment to make a major change. 'As it turned out there were a number of specific factors which all had a combination of behavioural and cognitive elements, which we then systematically started putting strategies in place to remedy' Greg explained. The elegance in this approach is that it highlights how much of an impact we can have on an individual's life when we remove what Greg describes as 'assumption based decision making'. I am confident that in some area of our life we have played out a confirmation bias, only to realise later on that we made a mistake. A confirmation bias is a simple partial mindset we take when we assume someone will act in a certain way. When the individual displays behaviours which meet our expectation we mentally reward ourselves for 'picking it' while when the individual displays behaviours which are contrary to our expectation we either:

» Minimise the interpretation and excuse that behaviour as an abnormality or,
» Reinterpret the behaviour so it appears that they are still acting consistently with the expectation.

Greg's approach is a very cognitive based style of leadership in which he systematically works through the situation applying, checking and continually re-assessing it to ensure he is achieving the best possible outcome.

Greg has spoken about times when he saw other leaders make

mistakes and the impact of those mistakes on the team and its ability to function. It is always a tricky area when it comes to commenting on your peers and most organisations shy away from really providing peer based feedback. We are comfortable with 360 degree anonymous and leader to direct report feedback but the peer to peer is often lacking. Greg was very conscious of this and suggested that it was an important element of leadership he had incorporated into his leadership style. He referred to this as "the tough love" component and said 'If an individual is not happy with their title or their remuneration, for example, and are often appearing to be very unmotivated, I often see leaders shying away from the "but that's just the way it is" conversation'. He went on to expand by saying, 'Leaders can often take on a parking officer's approach to the situation and impact the level of motivation in the person'. Greg suggested that they become very prescriptive in their approach and start to look at the actions of the individual so that they can explain in some way why they are in that situation (confirmation bias raising its ugly head again). In other words, 'let's look for all the signs I can use to play back to that person as to why they are not performing'.

Using a more specific example, consider a leader who has been tasked with counselling a staff member who was unmotivated and somewhat disgruntled with their level of pay, or the seniority of their role. There are a number of ways this could be handled but the following is one I have seen play out all too often. The leader responded to this person by saying 'let me show you all the grammatical errors on your last report you submitted' and then followed it up by telling them their decision making at this point was severely lacking in foresight. It appears that the individual was attempting to justify why their direct report was at that level and by inference suggested that if they worked harder they could get promoted. Greg's response to that example was quiet insightful, 'what they failed to realise is the reality of the situation, which is the need for the individual to perform exceptionally at their role, regardless of their desire to get promoted'. We need to start reversing the conversation and focus the individual on what is needed within a job, while still highlighting the promotion opportunities, as opposed to focusing on exceeding expectations outside of the position and then expecting a promotion. Organisations can only be truly successful if everyone is performing exceptionally, which suggests that we need to ensure we have the right people in the right role. The challenge leaders often face is when they have an individual who is in the wrong role and they are forced to try and motivate them to perform effectively within it. The bad news is that even with the best intent you will ultimately fail. So how do you minimise this impact? Greg relates this point back to his comment on tough love and authenticity when he suggests that, "sometimes you just need to have that tough conversation with an individual and layout the reality of the situation and the options ahead".

So how do leaders motivate when organisations often tie performance into a scorecard based formula and in Greg's case also link his remuneration to the outcome of his team?

'Imagine a situation where I stand up in front of my 140 odd staff and say, "OK everyone we really need to hit these targets so I can get paid"'. Greg reflects on a couple of possible outcomes from that statement:

» There may be a few who think that I'm a nice guy and will actively work hard to make that happen.
» The bulk probably won't care.

It was very clear from his comments that the focus here was not to try and convince people of what they should be doing but in fact create an environment in which they wanted to expel their discretionary effort, be engaged, achieve outcomes and most importantly feel personally rewarded for their own effort. 'There always has to be something in it for each person'. Greg reflected, because if there isn't, then all he has to rely on is good will, 'and let's be honest that is not going to work in the long term'. 'I am consistently challenging myself to ensure that I am inspiring my team to want to be their best'. Greg's challenge is that organisations often limit the levers a leader has; Ben Lawrence (See page152) refers to the need for organisations to allow leaders to say yes as easily as it expects them to say no. How do we inspire our staff and what levers can we pull? The motivational continuum highlights how a different mindset will drive the person to react very differently to a variety of stimuli. This added level of complexity makes life very difficult for leaders like Greg who have large teams where each member will be motivated in ways that are dissimilar. Greg discussed the concept of stretch targets and how many organisations use them to motivate staff to work harder and may receive an additional bonus if they are successful. On the surface this appears to make sense and may actually work for some but for an individual who is in the motivated to avoid failure mindset, the concept of a stretch target may actually produce a decrease in performance and a completely opposite attitude to what you expected.

How can a stretch target actually result in a decrease in performance?

Consider the classic example of the individual being placed in a position where they could be stretched. The problem here is that the method used to stretch the individual was to remove them from their current job (in which they were excelling) and place them into a completely new part of the business and expect them to perform at the same level. The more concerning part is that they are then given negative feedback if/when their performance drops off.

This situation captures the motivational mindset in action perfectly.

It would not take too much imagination to predict the behaviour of this person should they have stayed in the new role. In fact, I would argue that the motivation to avoid failure mindset could have stayed, even when they returned to their old position, in an attempt to regain their performance level. The net effect is that the individual is likely to head back to their old position, reduce their desire to be flexible, shy away from any other development opportunities and may very likely choose not to stick their neck out for the organisation again. A secondary effect of this situation is that other people in the team on seeing this outcome may become somewhat reticent about being 'stretched'.

The final piece to Greg's puzzle is the makeup of his team. 'I am absolutely focused on diversity and inclusion in my teams and by diversity I don't mean only gender. Diversity to me is about experience and length of that experience, range of experience, diversity of thought and perspective'. At this stage, I recalled a leadership workshop I facilitated for Greg two years prior, when he first assumed the role of CIA, the workshop consisted of all his direct reports, most of whom were long-term auditors. He commented 'today my team is vastly different from that initial team, and I am proud of the fact that the original team have moved upwards in their career and most are still within the bank. I even have a new member of my team who used to be a journalist!' You have to admire a leader who has found a way to bring a journalist into an auditing role, but then again when you consider the skills of a journalist and the requirements of an auditor to uncover the story and the focus on customer advocacy, you can understand why. According to Greg 'the Audit Board has also been extremely complimentary on the diversity of the team'. So maybe he is onto to something here.

During that earlier workshop, Greg commented to me that his goal was to create an environment, in which his people became the ones poached by the business and not the other way round. He has clearly achieved this one.

Greg has clearly articulated how much time he spends honing his leadership skills and after everything we discussed I asked him to summarise his thoughts as a lead into the take home section of this chapter.

> *I need to be motivated myself and that starts with really checking in with myself and being very honest about what I am thinking and how I am feeling. I love my job, I love this organisation, I love what I do and that makes a massive difference; especially on the tough days. What it also enables me to do is to challenge myself everyday on what I am trying to achieve and how I can re-energise myself when I need to. This approach can also then be extended onto my team. I am very conscious of the shadow I am casting into my team and the impact it has on them; the business results will follow. Regardless of what is said about hierarchies and no matter how flat a structure you try to create, the perception of a hierarchy will always be present and the mindset or even mood state of a leader can directly or indirectly impact on the team.*

TAKE HOME

» Everyone really is different and you need to take the time to understand this. Only they can choose to give you their discretionary effort.

» Process based goals are more effective – let the results look after themselves.

» One person's stretch target may prove to be another's death target.

» Plan your interactions; don't just have a meeting off the cuff.
» Consider how you provide feedback and the frame of reference you are using. Is the outcome most important versus the continual development perspective?
» Where possible ensure all conversations are held with a solid reality check. Remember everyone has a role to play to ensure success.
» Love what you do. It's going to be hard to sustain it of you don't.
» Understand the impact you have on your organisation and your people and respect it.

ROD LEAVER
Chief Executive Officer, Lendlease Asia

Rod Leaver was appointed Chief Executive Officer Asia in April 2011, and is currently based in Singapore.

He joined Lendlease in January 2008. Prior to his current role, Rod was Chief Executive Officer Australia and before this Chief Executive Officer of Asia Pacific and Global Head of Lendlease's investment management business, where he also had responsibility for the UK infrastructure development business and the US based public partnership's business.

Rod has extensive experience in the property investment and funds management industry. He previously held roles as Executive Chairman and founder of the listed Ronin Property Group, managing total funds of AUD$2.4 billion. He co-founded and worked as Chief Executive Officer of the listed property investment company, James Fielding Group, managing total funds of AUD$1.8 billion and was also a co-founder and Executive Director of Paladin Australia Limited, managing total funds of AUD$2.3 billion.

Rod is currently a member of the Singapore Government's Urban Redevelopment Authority's Design Advisory Committee and the Regional Director Asia of the Global Foundation. He served as a Director of the Green Building Council of Australia; is a member of the Australian Government's Business Roundtable on Climate Change, a National Director of the Property Council of Australia and was its New South Wales President for three years. He has also held positions as Chair of the Australian National Business Leader's Forum on Sustainable Development and sat on the New South Wales Government's Heritage Council and their Historic Houses Trust Foundation as well as the Property Industry Foundation. He is also a Fellow of the Australian Property Institute and a Fellow of the Royal Institute of Chartered Surveyors.

I recall a fascinating conversation with Rod soon after he took on the role as the CEO Lendlease Asia. We were discussing leadership and how companies structure themselves to achieve their desired outcome. Rod smiled at one point, sat back in his chair and reflected that in his time at Lendlease, which was only four years at this stage, he had already had four different jobs, albeit all starting with the CEO title. Several years later, while giving thought to his role in Singapore, he was quite introspective on the challenges working in Asia brings.

> *I think it's really a challenging but interesting scenario for the Lendlease business across Asia on how you motivate or inspire people because we actually operate across four very different countries. You've got China, Japan, Malaysia, and Singapore. And you've got teams on the ground in each of those countries and many of them in different disciplines, from construction, development, and investment management to all the functional support services. There's nothing homogenous about this business at all and therefore when you look at how you run this business and how you get messages through, it's extremely challenging as you cannot send the same message across the whole business.*

Rod added another challenge, which many international companies may face.

'For international companies, many of the policies and procedures are set at the global level. Our global head office is in Australia, so sometimes the content may be Australian centric and from an Australian perspective. You need to be extremely aware and take efforts to customise them for Asia and ensure that they are equally relevant locally'.

From Rod's perspective the most important element is 'actually thinking about the audience and their needs; if you want to motivate them or get them moving then how do you actually translate the message to reflect that, and I don't mean just translate it from English to Japanese, I mean from a cultural perspective'.

Rod's strategy is not an external one of 'getting the translation right' or 'delivering in a specific way'. He focuses on his own self-awareness, which he describes as 'the first place to start. It's understanding the fact that we don't have all the answers and we need to think about and understand the complexities of that culture, the history of that country, why it is the way it is and not judge it and say it's wrong. This will allow you to give a more comprehensive perspective around a better message'. He expanded on this concept by considering the type and style of messages you send, 'emails are very different from voicemails, while verbal presentations are again interpreted differently from written newsletters. Everything's got to be reviewed over and over; you do get better at this as you begin to understand it. But you need to stop and think'. I am sure many of you are thinking, 'that's all well and good but I simply don't have the time to spend on all these idiosyncrasies'. This too is a reality for Rod who has seen it all when it comes to operating under pressure.

> *As an international company, our clients benefit from our wealth of global knowledge combined with local expertise, we have amazing talent recruited from all around the region and the world. We work in small client centric*

teams who are often under a lot of pressure. Now you add in that additional crosscultural pressure, with a net effect of some individuals reverting to their upbringing and their culture. It can create a lot of tension if not managed well. So the key is to provide awareness of different cultures that will encompass different working styles and structure.

So does a company's values fall in line with the culture, or should the culture fall in line with the company values? I am not convinced there is a right or wrong answer to that question, and I am sure there are examples where both sides of the argument have shown to be effective. Lendlease has taken a perspective and believes consistency in the message will bind all its employees regardless of their locations. 'The thing that binds us all together and how we work through the tough times is really having a clear purpose. We need a higher purpose around the business that transcends the culture of China, of Japan and even Australia, it's the culture of Lendlease and this is what's expected'. This higher sense of purpose is the approach Rod and his fellow senior leaders use for inspiration. He maintains that one of his most used strategies is simply talking about why Lendlease exists and what they are trying to achieve. 'You're working for a great company, driven by a very strong set of principles and values. Our principles of safety, sustainability, diversity and customer focus are all driven for respect of people and the environment and cultures we work in. Our values, are well defined by the behaviours that we expect of our people'. He expects his people to demonstrate those values in all their workplace dealings regardless of their cultural background. 'I expected them to collaborate, to have respect for one another, have upmost integrity, have trust in the organisation and build trust with our clients'.

Not a lot to do but one could argue these values and principles have guided the business for well over 50 years and it does not appear that they will be stepping down from this perspective any time soon.

Working in a large organisation that is steeped in history can be daunting for any executive, especially those who did not start in the graduate program but were lateral hires higher up the organisational chart. Rod in his many years has seen very talented people simply not make it, regardless of their aspirations to work for a company. 'When you go to work for Apple or you go to work for Virgin, you know exactly what kind of company you're going to work for. You might have an aspiration to go and work at those companies. But unless you're a good fit to that culture, you'd be chewed up and spat out pretty quickly. There are many companies I wouldn't go to work for because I know what their culture is driven by'. From Rod's perspective, Lendlease has created an environment driven by 'doing great things and building great communities enabling people to enhance their lives'. This may sound utopic but it is the consistent anchor Rod reminds all his staff about as often he can.

> *I would put this question to all my staff, why should they be motivated to get out of bed every morning and go to work? If it's a drudge and they're not inspired to do that, there's no passion and I'm sure they would be looking for a new job in due course. There is a plethora of reasons why people become unmotivated and disengaged from an organisation. Our tough times can be very challenging due to the long time frame required to seal a deal, and this can disengage some people. Our job as leaders is to make sure that they stay highly engaged and through the tough times. They need to believe that we're on the right course, we've got the right strategy and we're employing the best people.*

Part of Rod's strategy is to ensure that he is touching the business well below his senior executive level.

> *From a personal perspective, I have now actually taken to having one on one conversation with individuals from all around the business. I'm doing 50 of those a year, understanding what the needs are. You get out of touch with what's going on in a large business and all of a sudden you're going off on one path and the rest of the business just says, 'well you don't understand what our problems are'. An important part of being able to allow them to feel as if they've got a connection and a voice to be able to say, 'I've got concerns'. In this day and age with social media, everyone has a voice, but companies generally don't. It's a one-way communication from top down, as opposed to allowing bottom up interaction.*

Rod's 50 one on one's include the most junior people on site through to individuals from all levels in the business. 'I need to make sure the message is getting through, it's probably the most important thing I actually do. And, can I say, it's nothing about me talking. It's actually me asking questions and listening and it's amazing how open the individuals are about the challenges they face day to day'.

We often look to some of the great companies around and try to understand what and how they do things that have made them successful. I believe we are actually asking the wrong question. What and how a company operates is a valid set of questions but not the most important one. The most important question a company should answer is:

Why does it exist?

Rod and I spent time discussing the pros and cons of a number of very successful companies in particular Apple and Virgin and their respective creators Steve Jobs and Richard Branson. In his own words, he would 'not dare put myself in comparison to either of those rock stars, however from a personal perspective I aim to employ very capable people around me and ensure they understand why we are here. They need to be passionate and that means they will often have their own why but as long as it is aligned to our overarching anchor, I know I am onto someone great'. Rod expanded on the influence of Jobs and Branson.

> *He (Jobs) created a company that is focused on the customer; the financial results are the bi-product of getting everything else right. They just happen to be the most valuable company in the world, so they must be doing something right. I think Virgin is exactly the same, as long as you focus on the customer and ensure you are meeting their needs, your chances of developing a very long standing sustainable company is almost guaranteed – although you still need a great product or service. I think Lendlease does that, we focus on the needs of the customer in their community and that drives everything that we do. We create great places that meet their needs however we always have to stay on top of meeting their needs and staying relevant to them. As opposed to being inward looking, which is all about us'.*

But what about the money? It is important that companies still get a return on their investment and Lendlease is no different. However, I would argue that they would more than likely walk away from a deal that would make a huge return if it was going to violate their key values and principles. Rod commented 'when it comes to safety, we are uncompromising, as it should be along with our other principles around sustainability, diversity and customer focus. So the customer either is aligned with us on our values and therefore making sure everyone goes home safe every day, or quite frankly they are not our clients'. He was very adamant that his approach is focused on building long-term relationships with clients. However he still recognised that making a financial return is a part of overall sustainability. 'If our clients are not making a return in line with their expectations, then they are unlikely to return or maintain their own sustainability, so we need to include this in our balancing act'. Rod took a leaf out of the Branson mantra and was very passionate about the need to ensure you have a strong brand. 'they created the powerful brand of 'Virgin' and that in itself helps them to continue to be successful. Brand and reputation are derived from what you do as a business and how you go about doing it'. So being able to walk the talk on your values and stay true and uncompromising to your principles is really about defining the company and therefore its brand.

That being said, they are clearly still doing incredibly well and at the time of writing this book, Rod had secured several billion dollars in projects and one was in the final throws of being signed off on.

Rod's final words when questioned on what gets him out of bed.

> *I think the fact that I've been in real estate my whole working career and I love seeing amazing places that just work for people and that's what Lendlease creates. I've worked in my own businesses previously. But when you've got a whole machine made up of such a talented team that has track record and credibility globally and then you have*

the opportunity to present that to governments and clients, it's amazing. I lead a team that develops large-scale community projects that are creating amazing places for people. Where else can you get that?

TAKE HOME

» There is no one-size-fits-all message. Think about the audience and their needs to customise your messaging.

» The importance of self-awareness of the cultural differences around the countries in which the company operates.

» A clear global and higher purpose that transcends cultures is useful in binding diverse group of employees.

» Have conversations deep into the business, not just your direct reports. The deeper you go the richer the content becomes.

» Your brand is vital; understand it and how it impacts others.

JOHN DURKAN
Managing Director – Coles

John Durkan is Managing Director of the Coles Group. Coles is a food, grocery, liquor and convenience retailer that serves over 19 million customers each week, employs over 100,000 team members and operates with thousands of suppliers. John joined Coles in July 2008 as Merchandise Director and was subsequently appointed Chief Operating Officer in June 2013. John has added a wealth of customer, product and buying knowledge to Coles having worked for 17 years with Safeway Stores PLC in the UK, a large-scale food retailer that operates supermarkets, convenience and fuel outlets. Prior to that, he was the Chief Operating Officer for Carphone Warehouse, the UK's largest independent mobile phone retailer. That business spans 10 European countries with a fast-paced and strong entrepreneurial culture—one that John is committed to enabling at Coles.

When you walk into the Coles head office you cannot help but notice the overt way they express their values and achievements. The walls are draped with examples of savings and upcoming specials and on the large TV screen is a video playing highlighting the support they have given to both individuals and communities through grants and the like. John's office was like everyone else's and situated up on one of the floors in an open plan layout. Like his photo above, he looks relaxed and has an air of confidence, which was evident throughout our interview.

Imagine you have just received the call from the CEO of Wesfarmers to inform you of your successful appointment as the CEO of Coles, where do you start? 'To give you some context, we have over 100,000 team members, so quite a sizeable army. Sometimes we think of it as an army, and think of how we might motivate and get people moving in the same direction. Because effectively, that's what we've got to do'. So where is his focus? 'What we're really looking for, ultimately, is consistency. What we've got is 2,200 shops if I take all of our Coles, Liquor and Coles express businesses. We need to have absolute consistency in the customer experience across those businesses and you do have to think of it as motivating an army of people because you want 100 thousand people marching in the same direction'. Getting this army of people all marching in the same direction is a challenge many of us face, the numbers may not always be as high but the challenge is still the same. We know through research conducted in the eye witness testimony arena, that when ten people are asked to witness an event and then recall the facts from the situation, very few will be able to recall the facts consistently with others. This differentiation occurs as we don't always process information the same way, in most cases our biases and assumptions play a significant role in filling in the gaps and can often lead us to interpret a situation very differently.

John recognises that his people will interpret his strategy in different ways and has deliberately taken a simple perspective.

You've got to have a clear end goal; supported by a clear strategy and that everybody in the organisation can feel motivated to get behind. For me that's about putting our customers first, second and third. It is as simple as that. Additionally I want to ensure we are continually lowering prices, providing a really strong fresh offer and ensuring that we provide great customer service every day of the year.

John's goal in this approach is to encourage his staff to think about how they do that. To help, the senior leadership team 'Came up with a strap line that we put under our logo called:

A little better every day.

Now it's really simple for everyone to get that and say 'you know what, I can do something with that, I can be a little better every day. And if I'm going to be a little better every day, what's my version of that?'

The idea of a little better everyday aligns perfectly to an analogy I regularly use. I shared this with John to gain his further interpretation of what a 'little better' actually meant.

> *Here is a story that illustrates very well the process of setting goals, and what can be achieved when you set them properly. I was having a conversation with a male swimming athlete. He turned up at my office indicating he was not happy with the progress of his swimming and wanted to win the state championships in two years' time. It became very clear that this was a determined young man and while he had a solid set of long-term goals, including making the Olympic Team for the Beijing Olympics, he was very light on his short-term goals. We started discussing what he needed to do to achieve his goal of winning the state championships. It came down to simply shaving four seconds off his personal best for the 100 metres freestyle. For any non-swimmers reading this, four seconds in the pool is no mean feat, especially over 100 metres. To cut the rest of the story short, while a goal of shaving four seconds was very ambitious and daunting, 0.0035 seconds wasn't. Where does the 0.0035 seconds come from? Well,*

he trained six days per week for forty-eight weeks in the year—totalling 288 sessions. On each day he trained twice, giving a total of 576 sessions per year. Over a two-year period he had a grand total of 1,152 sessions before the next state championships. By dividing his four seconds by 1,152 sessions, we got a goal of shaving 0.0035 seconds per training session. His long-term goal suddenly became very achievable. Two years later not only did he win the state championships, but he shaved almost 4.1 seconds off his personal best.

Here is John's take on it.

If I take these stores, we don't focus them on the output. We don't say that we want to be x million better of this year or we want to be y million better that quarter. Of course at some point we bring metrics into it, but we don't start with that. We start with the idea that if we're going to have better prices than everywhere else, a better service mentality, fresher product, better in store availability, it's likely that we're going to get more shoppers shopping with us. And if you're a team member, working on our checkout, you want to know that we're going to give you all the tools that you need, to be able to deliver that to every customer every time. I really don't think our team members in the stores spend a lot of their time worrying about the profit and loss statement and the predicted revenue figures the board is interested in. They want to go home to their families feeling like they have contributed to something. I just need to allow them to contribute and connect with the message.

When you look back at Part one of the book, you may recall the sentiment I posited that a corporation could really only inspire, it's up to the individual to be motivated. John's simple and consistent strategy is that 'we've got to set the right environment —we want people to get out of bed every day and go to work and say, I really want to be here'. John and his team have extended 'a little bit better every day' to his store managers as well. This group was historically held accountable for the metrics of their store and were rewarded based on those KPIs being achieved. This approach is now also falling in line with his overall strategy.

> *I want our store managers and their teams to be empowered to trade. After all, they're the ones serving our customers and they're the ones who have the knowledge and experience to present the best possible customer offer. I see the role of the head office as one of supporting stores – not telling them what to do. Our goal in our Store Support Centre is to take away the barriers and bureaucracy for our stores and give them the tools they need to succeed.*

The elegance in this strategy is that store managers are now accountable for an area of the business they actually have some control over. The old adage of 'control the controllable', which has been around for years, but is rarely used, looks like it has some traction within the Coles structure. We need to consider why an insight, which on the surface is obviously sound 'control what you can control and disregard the rest', appears to fail when moved into common practice. Why would we focus in on elements that are out of our control and ones, which often lead to interpretations of failure? The motivational continuum provides some insight into why. Consider this, individuals who are in the MTAF mindset and are evaluating their environment are likely to place more emphasis on the elements which contrite or predict failure even if those elements are out of one's control. The motivation then to avoid that failure, is so powerful that we start to believe we can interact with the 'uncontrollable' and maybe even alter it in some way. Logic and hindsight informs us to the likely answer but remember our emotional brain, which has no propensity for language, takes over and so begins the slippery slope downward.

In John's world, the creation of trust is paramount. He needed to find a mechanism that would break through the individual's gut interpretation of the situation. I would argue that a likely interpretation by a store manager when they first heard their KPI's were less metric and more behavioural might have been one with a degree of scepticism. John was adamant that trust was the key.

> *I think you need to trust team members that they are doing the right things, that they are well intentioned and motivated. That's got to be the starting point. I see too many organisations that take the opposite approach to their team and it shows - in their culture and ultimately their results.*
>
> *I want our team to feel trusted when they come to work. They need to have clear accountability in their role and no ambiguity in their responsibilities. Then collectively, we need to work hard to correct the things that go wrong but never forget to regularly celebrate the things that go right.*

But how do you reward someone when it's hard to measure 'little things'?

> *Rewarding people is important, but this isn't just financial reward, it's rewarding people to say that was a great job. Recognising them by doing that is unbelievably motivating! I'll give you an example—in the last year we ran a program in Coles called Community Hero. We went out to every single team member across the organisation and asked them for their stories about what they do in the local community that we didn't know about. We had floods of stories of team members going way beyond what you'd expect of them in the local community, outside of their Coles commitment. We held regional finals, state finals and then the national finals. Here, we recognised all the work that had been done by all these team members, and it's just a way of saying what we do within our community is more important, or at least equally important, to what we do within the walls and we want to recognise it. That builds a whole lot of good will and gives Coles a personality that says this is the sort of organisation that I want to work for.*

Coles like many organisations are on a journey and we often hear the word culture being bandied about, usually within the context of 'changing the culture'. While I could spend an entire book discussing the concept of a culture, which is for another time, what I will say is that:

Culture eats strategy for breakfast any day of the week.

- Peter Drucker

The more important question to ask yourself is 'who and how is a culture set and how does that culture impact on the motivation of its team to deliver?' John was the first to suggest that culture is front of mind for him but that 'this is a long journey for us. We're right at the start of it - and with 101,000 team members across Australia - it's certainly a challenge. But I think we've made a good start'. I questioned John as to whether his approach of 'a little better every day' changed its focus when he was working with his immediate team.

> 'Not really. The cultural piece is really important and I think it starts for me and us around that table. So behaving and acting in the same way and messaging in the same way is quite important. And they have no more or no less metrics than the team in the shop. They're not exactly the same metrics. But the quantity of metric is quite small. Again, it's all inputs for us, not outputs. It's how we think about being customer first in everything that we do. We start with that and then think 'okay, I work in different divisions, if I'm going to be a little better every day, what's my version of a little better every day in my division? How am I going to deliver that? And how am I going to be bold and take responsibility and accountability and our aim is to empower the organisation?' So our aim is not decision making all at the top. We want to push because

really where we want the decision to be taken and that is out is in stores. How am I going to say what's required in stores in Western Australia, in Kununurra or Broome? Or even Warrnambool here in Victoria. The best people are the people on the ground that are going to make those decisions. So there's a lot more of self-motivation that goes on at the more senior level where people are much more driven, clearly high achievers, self-starters and we pick our team to be those sorts of individuals. I've looked for people who demonstrate these attributes. I'm going to be a self- starter, I'm going to be hungry for what I want to do, I want to make Coles the best retailer in Australia. Therefore, it's easier to motivate people because you're giving them the freedom to operate. Not micromanaging. Allowing that group of people to be trusted and have the accountability they require in the organisation, and I want that at all levels.

Many CEO's face the same dilemma that John is inherently describing here. They cannot do all the work; they have to rely on their people delivering on the values and goals on their behalf. If we talk the talk and don't then walk the walk, we very quickly can create an environment, which promotes the MTAF mindset. 'We've got to walk the talk in this place. It's really quite important. It's important that we do it and we're seen to do it, so we live what we say, because otherwise it's just words on a piece of paper. And they become irrelevant and people ignore them'. John's strategy aligns perfectly to the commentary of Ben Lawrence (Wesfarmers Head of HR) who stated that the Wesfarmers model was to allow each business to operate under its own accountability model and for the leaders to have the power to say YES as well as the power to say NO.

> *I have the luxury of choosing my team and therefore I have a great deal of belief that these are the right people and if I believe that they're the right people, then I need to trust them that they're going to be able to do the job and not micromanage them. Because that's the worst thing that could happen (micromanage them). At that point it does become demotivational to come into work, if you're not going to have a leader who just wants to get on with it. 'Let's drive, let's go!' I couldn't think of anything worse than a leader who has to continually check in with management that it's OK to do something.*

CEO's are expected and required to hold the ultimate accountability for their respective organisations, but you have to wonder how they motivate themselves. Different leaders all have their own approaches, which are all slightly different but also have some common themes. John's is no different.

> *I don't know about anyone else, but for me, there's a drive and an energy about being able to make food in Australia more affordable for our customers and I look at it from the point of view that says, this is a company that's 100 years old, it has a long history and I'm simply a temporary guardian of the business. My job is to make sure that it continues to be sustainable and have longevity. My view of that is that if we can make quality food more affordable for Australians, I would have looked after this business during my period of time. Now, there's a huge motivation in that*

for me, which is way beyond running a business, in that I can look myself in the mirror every day and ask are we achieving that? And in that respect it means that I spring out of bed and I've got an energy around this business.

This approach did not develop overnight for John.

I think it goes back to how I was brought up and my motivation for doing what I do. I never expected or thought that I would be given the opportunity to run a business like this. And all the jobs that I've had throughout my career, I've never gone, you know, in five years' time I need to be doing this or in ten years' time I need to be doing that. Has not even crossed my mind. Not planned in any way, shape or form. I lost my parents at a relatively early age and therefore I took one day at a time or one week at a time, at most six months to a year. I didn't look any further than that. I have always thought you know what? I've got to make the most of this. I've got to give it a go. There's no point being half in or half out. There's no point just going to work for a job. I go because I can do something different; I can make a difference.

We often find that our upbringing, the circumstances we face as young men and women often craft who we become later in life. We learn very early on how to deal with success and failure and these messages are often supported by those we surround ourselves with. Our motivation to succeed and subsequent motivation to avoid failure will almost always anchor itself to the sum of our experiences. This however, presents us with a wonderful opportunity to take control of how we choose to act and choose to be motivated. While our past may infer a response to a current event, it is still a combination of our emotional and logical brain, which determines our final action.

John, on dealing with failure:

> *It's the same way I deal with success, in fact. It's exactly the same, if you get carried away with your success or become too despondent about your failure, they're the same sort of impediment, if you like. You just got to be resilient and not go down into a hollow, worry about it and get demoralised. It's about saying, "well we've failed, I've failed, and you know what? I've learnt from it, we'll pick ourselves up and we'll carry on going." And when we're really successful, we say, "well we've been okay and we need to do better." You can't be either in my view. You have to be balanced in all of this.*

John's final thoughts on the topic referred to his business as he contemplated how the concept of failure is often perceived in business. 'One of the things here we're always grappling with is how do we allow failure to happen and pick people up because it's a hell of a difficult task. People normally feel that they're going to be criticised, or even worst penalised, for failing'.

It's always easier to manage how you respond to failure or success, the goal here is to transfer that insight into your wider sphere of influence. Imagine a world where it was OK to fail some of the time, maybe even encouraged to fail just to learn. Think about a world where you still kept your job or received praise for trying. I believe we have the capacity to understand this; we just seem to fall short in the application of it. I hope that this and all the other chapters have given you some insights into what is possible. We just need to action it and believe in it.

TAKE HOME

» Consistency needs to be delivered at all levels in the business.

» The customer is the best indicator of your value system and its penetration through the business. They will vote with their feet!

» Keep it simple.

» Allow your team to achieve through your vision; they need to create the path though.

» Break goals down into sizeable chunks.

» Trust has to be your starting point.

» Be a little better every day.

NOEL CONDON
CEO – AIG

Noel Condon was appointed CEO and director of AIG Australia Limited in August 2010. He joined AIG as a marine underwriter in 1984 in his hometown of Dublin, Ireland. Since then, he has held a variety of underwriting, marketing and country management roles in the UK, Europe, Asia and New Zealand. Prior to his most recent appointment, he was based in Brussels as Country Manager for AIG's operations in Belgium and Luxembourg. Noel was appointed Head of Country Operations for Australasia in September 2013.

Corporate insurance companies are well known for not being well known. We see the outward advertising of personal insurance companies which are directed towards individuals and focused on how they are there to support you, when either you or someone else, does something stupid. Whichever way, someone needs to pay for the mistake and that is when the insurance company becomes very relevant. From a corporate perspective, you almost never see any advertising and very little promotion of the services offered. When it comes to institutional insurance, the name of the game is relationship and value proposition. The most successful insurance companies are ones who not only have great offers, but also understand how to share risk and minimise the hit to their bottom line when claims come through. Price, while important, is not always top of the list. For Noel, this is his day-to-day challenge. How does his team continually maintain relationships with their direct and indirect clients? How does he continue to inspire his team to look for new and innovative approaches to selling more insurance policies?

We're in about 75 countries around the world. With Australia ranking probably about number eight or nine in terms of top line. Our number of employees is about 400 all up, with top line revenue of about 550 million dollars and growing. We are mainly in the industrial commercial insurance space focusing on commercial industrial property insurance, construction, oil and petrochemical mining accounts. We're also a big player in profession indemnity, director's and officer's indemnity insurance. Those two classes of businesses, property and financial lines we call it, would represent about 70 per cent of our top line premium, while our supporting lines of revenue come from liability insurance, environmental insurance, and cargo on the move. Finally we have some innovative offers including high net worth, personal property and travel insurance. If you go onto Jetstar's website, you'll find travel insurance from AIG. And actually, more recently, if you walk into an Apple store, buy a product and take the insurance? That's us.

It is amazing to see how the concept of insurance has been disrupted over the years, when you consider its beginning in the shipyards of London in the early 17th century. It was during this time that some entrepreneurs recognised that ship owners would want some protection for the cargo they were transporting around the world. The concept of insurance hasn't changed but the climate is continually developing and the level of risk companies are prepared to tackle on is phenomenal. If I were to pick an industry that speaks to the motivational continuum, the closest would be insurance companies. Their basic principle is to not fail, that is, don't take on risk that they cannot cover. One could imagine that an individual who is motivated to avoid failure may struggle to be successful in an insurance career, while individuals who simply take on too much risk would also struggle to succeed. Definitely a balancing act. The other consideration is that insurance is one of very few professions for which there is no need for a degree to enter. Many insurance brokers choose to educate themselves, but it is not a requirement to enter the profession. This leads to quite a diverse group of individuals choosing to enter the profession. Over the years with tertiary education becoming more prevalent, the makeup of individuals in insurance companies is quite distinct.

Noel is very cognisant of this and recognised that:

> *We have probably 25 per cent of our workforce in the 50+ bracket. Quite a lot of wise old owls in the business. We do have a big group of young people coming up through the business; the youth in our business under 30 represents about 40 per cent of our workforce. I think we have been able to recruit a diverse group of people because, in my view, we don't care what age we are and we never have cared what age people are. If you've got the skill set, you've got the ambition and a little bit of experience, we'll give you authority and responsibility to go and do things. You want to travel? AIG is a fantastic way to be able to do it.*

Given the size of the organisation and the need to continually service clients, Noel has taken a specific perspective when it comes to the overall focus of his team. The greatest change he has overseen has been the operations of the back office. The way he sees it the concept of the 'back office' or better known as the 'claims department' doesn't really exist anymore.

I do not classify claims operations as back office. It's very front office and that has been a huge change that we've enacted here, in terms of how we think about claims. We acknowledge what our claims people do, and respect the contribution they make to the company. Much of our administration work happens offshore, therefore just about everybody is forward market facing, but they're not just in sales. We have a number of roles which are not overtly client facing however, for example, if you're an underwriter pricing risk, but we still want you in the market place and engaging with our clients.

The effect of Noel's approach has been that everyone in the business understands the impact risk and how the business needs to operate to be effective. He was very particular in his views on why he sees the whole team as forward facing.

Insurance is what we sell, but the world is changing. There's an interesting dynamic between insurance brokers and sellers of insurance. A corporation goes to the broker, the broker accesses the market and makes a decision, this is who we want to insure the risk and this is where we are going to place your business. Generally speaking, the client does not need their insurer until there's a claim. That's how it was in the past. When the claim happened, you could potentially feel exposed. Not that they've done anything wrong, but they just have this moment where they think 'I really hope the insurance company comes through and does what it says it was going to do in the first place'.

The insurance industry has significantly changed over the past 10 years according to Noel.

> *Unhappy and dissatisfied brokers have led to institutions continually re-evaluating their insurance policies, particularly when claims were made and the broker perceived a mistake was made in the placement of the insurance.*
>
> *We have encouraged our claims department to be more proactive, more affirmative, and step up, rather than hide in the corner and wait to be dragged into a court room or a mediation. In the dim and distant past, paying a claim as a claims handler was stressful, you might be sitting on a maximum reserve for that claim, of 500 thousand dollars, but you've settled it for 560 thousand dollars due to the particular circumstances. You might think 'wow I'm going to get into trouble for doing that'. Generally speaking, you try to settle within reserve, but I think what we have now is a situation where claims people want to set the correct reserves but they also want to do the right thing by the broker and the client, whatever the reserve might be.*

The overarching goal from Noel's perspective is to provide assurance to his team that they have the responsibility to make the best decision for both the client and the company. While this all seems very complex, the underlying principle lends itself beautifully to the mindset of motivation to avoid failure. In the past, individuals were highly motivated to avoid failure and therefore would act in particular ways to ensure the outcome was in their favour, or worst case they were dragged into a court in which the excuse mechanism was built, 'It wasn't my fault the arbitrator made a decision'. Not paying a clam in full or pushing out the time to pay was very much part of the landscape, but that has changed.

Changing the perspective of clients on the role of insurance companies is very much front of mind for Noel.

> *There were some structural changes that needed to occur. In the past, AIG was a big buyer of reinsurance. So when we had a large claim, we would have to go to the reinsurers and inform them that we are going to be making a payment shortly. So for us to make a substantial payment and not be out of pocket ourselves, we would then make a cash call on the reinsurers. For example, a claim of 10 million dollars could include 6 million from the reinsurers. We would send them a bill and it takes time for that money to come to us. While we're doing that, clients and brokers perceive that we're delaying action.*
>
> *Today, in most cases and most claims of that size, it's all ours, we are no longer buying that same level of reinsurance. This allows us to make those decisions unilaterally. From a finance accounting perspective, if we have a claim reserve for 10 million, it sits there in our reserves. I can just as easily move it from the reserve column into the paid column.*

Noel recalled a major turning point in his thinking after being challenged by one of his major partners with the question, 'Why can't you pay claims faster?' He took this question back to his broader leadership team and facilitated a workshop specifically designed to answer the questions. The outcome of the workshop was the idea called 'Global Claims Promise'. Through the discussions of the workshop Noel and his team realised that 'we can actually pay faster and particularly on first party claims and property claims'. In real terms what this means is that where there is a claim and the independent loss adjuster provides us with an accurate dollar figure we can provide you a cheque for half of that estimate immediately

This approach is almost the opposite of the process many other global insurers took before. 'The first claim that we were able to use it on was in Australia. It was a factory underwater, we had the loss adjuster go in there 48 hours after the loss had occurred. He called our team in Melbourne and said, "it looks like an 8 million dollar material damage claim, but I still don't know what the business interruption piece is yet"'. In the past, the goal would have been to potentially sit on this claim for a period of time and reduce the impact on the bottom line. 'Our team member in Melbourne said thanks and executed a claim of 4 million that evening'.

To achieve this his staff required a significant amount of empowerment. 'Absolutely! All of our people in those positions have the authority to act accordingly.' In this case AIG was holding the insurance but the broker Marsh maintained the direct client interaction. 'We had paid 4 million dollars across to that particular Marsh client within 72 hours of the claim coming through. I think we even surprised Marsh and the client was obviously impressed. Four million dollars really helped dry out the company and get them back trading quicker than they could have ever imagined'.

AIG clearly decided to put their money where their mouth was and ensured that this new approach to paying out claims was not just a once off PR exercise. 'We even had the opportunity to do it again for that particular client about a year later'. What impressed Noel was how quickly the response was recognised by the business. 'I was amazed at how quickly that resonated through that company right up to the board level, they were absolutely delighted to receive that money so promptly from just one insurer, as they probably had ten other insurers also involved'.

Stories like that are powerful and highlight beautifully an environment that promotes a motivation to succeed mindset. Imagine how you would feel if you had recently joined AIG and heard this story internally. Stories are the most powerful mechanism a company has, to set and embed a culture and these types of stories are the most powerful. Noel and his team at AIG have gone beyond stating the intention and actually demonstrated the intent.

> *It's a fantastic feeling for somebody like me, who's been in the business for 30 years. I've seen what we were like in the past. We were the insurer hiding in the corner, sitting on our wallet, those days are gone, the feeling we get from actually being able to resolve a situation quickly and advance payment to an insurer, whether large or small, is fantastic. We know we are making a difference, and our claims people feel like they are being acknowledged for what they do.*

To maintain his message and ensure it filtered throughout the business, Noel instigated a number of activities, sharing one particular example. 'I started Good News Friday. It is just a series of bullet points as to who's done something noteworthy during the week'. For Noel, good news was any news he could share with the business and included work and personal titbits. Here are a few from the last couple of good news Friday blurbs.

» Somebody's had a baby.

» Somebody's won a new piece of business.

» Somebody's renewed a tough account under pressure.

» We've settled a claim in record time.

There are also times when something more extraordinary comes along and Noel maintained that he celebrates these with the same level of passion –'A good story is a good story'.

> *We had an extraordinary story recently where we had two people working on a project for a year and they managed to cut down the amount of commission that we were paying to business partners that had long since stopped being business partners. The outcome was a significant return straight to the bottom line. The team managed to achieve this without causing any grief; it was done sensitively, within the law and within the contract. I am very conscious of all our staff and treat all good news equally, all our colleagues who are paying claims promptly and sorting out substantial claims issues get a nod, not just on big ticket items like property, but also on our smaller claims like directors and officers or a marine claim, we're calling it out, and it feels great.*

Noel was very focused on how individuals join his business and the messages they receive, he was very cognisant of the fact that many people join his industry with some preconceived ideas.

> *I think our induction processes have improved but they're*

still nowhere near where I want them to be. I think we also need to be very flexible in how we deliver it, for example, a very experienced individual joined us in Melbourne and he didn't need induction into insurance, he just needed to walk around the office and meet a whole bunch of people including me. Others need almost a crash course in what and how we operate. They also need to understand what their colleagues in the other departments do – that's an important aspect. It's not everything and of course induction also includes a significant amount of time on technology. I think we need to take more time with it and actually immerse people in our style of doing business. I think they get most out of it when they watch their colleagues in action with brokers and feel that interaction that we have.

Nothing is more powerful than watching someone in action, you get to see the individual not just talk the talk but actually walk the walk. But this also has to apply to the leadership team. Recently, Noel was struck with a situation which obviously impacted on him significantly, as it still resonates with him a year or so later. He was walking into an elevator one day and a young lady greeted him, he responded in kind and introduced himself. Her response caught him off guard. 'Hi I am x and we have met before'. Noel recalls feeling awful and then realised that in fact while he had met her, he hadn't met many of the new team members and quickly decided to remedy the situation. 'I went to the senior leader of the group to let him know I was taking his team out to lunch'. Given this was not the norm, Noel clarified it was part of his new regime and that he was on a mission to get to know more of his staff. 'I wanted to get to know them and I did, it was fantastic, we had a lot of fun'. He quickly rattled off all the names of the people who joined him for lunch and felt very confident that by breaking down some of the barriers, he would further support his goal of collaboration. Without realising it, Noel was further enhancing the positive stories that would flow around the business.

It is often stated that the best indicator of your leadership is seen when you are not in the room.

Handling failure

Earlier, Noel discussed a situation in which a staff member felt empowered to settle on a claim, which had more zero's in it than most of us would see in a lifetime. It is important to re-iterate that in the insurance world, claims are usually seen as the negative side of an insurance business as they are the ones paying out—as opposed to the sales team who sell the products and bring in the revenue. Considering the motivational continuum, we can interpret the context and understand how a claims team-member could easily shift along towards the motivation to avoid failure. Noel was very aware of this situation and has attempted to ensure he has strategies throughout the business to overcome the slide. 'From a very senior level within the claims department globally, we have some extraordinary leaders. We have engaged this team with some of the greatest thinkers available to us in Europe and the US, such as Nobel prize winner, Daniel Kahnmen.

Daniel came and worked with our senior claims team to look at issues of reserving and claims paying. One of the outcomes of that was around the concept of anchoring a position. Anchoring has become a major focus for his teams and he shared an example of an individual who was particularly good at the process. 'He would put a goal on a board, and then everyone would rally around the board. He didn't force them to like it, or even agree with it but they had to focus on it and work to achieve it'.

'We at AIG recognise over the years that we have been pretty poor at this (anchoring)—we've been sitting up in the corner waiting for somebody else to call out a number. Why not actually pull out our own number? Why not be first out there? Why not be affirmative, take a position. Well now this is happening'. Noel was determined to role model the behavior he was expecting from his people and realised he was getting through to his company when one of his brokers was prepared to settle a claim that was 50 per cent above the companies reserve, but in the long term would likely save the company several multiples of the settling figure. Several years earlier this would simply never have happened.

Building a motivated culture in a section of your business which usually has a negative connotation attached to it is always problematic. For Noel it was his claims department, for no other reason than they are the team that pays out money not collect it.

Noel disclosed that he has utilised two strategies.

» First, show up in the department. It's not the dark black hole that it used to be viewed as, that 'oh no don't tell me about claims, it's negative'. I would show up in there, sit down and say 'You are an important cog in our high performing wheel'.
» Next, I insist on the claims manager speaking first during team

meetings. So I'll make some introductory comments for ten minutes or so, then I'll say, "OK claims, what's the good news?" And just bring them out of the shadows and into that front line, I think has made a difference.

The feedback Noel has received has all been positive and the claims department feels like a contributor to the overall strategy. The insight here is that we should never hide a part of our business simply because it appears on the surface to have a negative undertone.

Every CEO has their own specific strategies that they use and some of them a little quirky. Noel is no different and it comes down to how he likes receiving information. 'I've always said to people "Hey, if you want to give me bad news, I want it first thing in the morning. I can get used to the idea, I can think about communicating it, I can maybe call a broker and try to push it back, unwind it, but give it to me first thing in the morning". Good news I can take anytime'.

Understanding the insurance industry is not an easy task and at times I struggled to conceptualise exactly what they do and how it all comes together. But I am glad they exist and we all benefit from the protection they provide. That being said, Noel presented a number of strategies and initiatives we can all benefit from.

TAKE HOME

» Share your good news stories regardless of how small or potentially insignificant they may seem.

» Encourage others to also become your advocate for sharing great news stories.

» Get to know your people. It might be lots of dinners and coffees but it's worth it.

» Consider the name people use to describe themselves – changing a title can have a huge impact.

» Sometimes your biggest negative can become your greatest positive. Don't hide from a part of the business that appears to have a negative connotation attached to it. Bring them front and centre and celebrate their contrition to be the business.

» Recognise that inducting a person into your business needs to be personalised. One size does not fit all.

DR MICHAEL SCHAPER
Deputy Chairman – ACCC

Dr Michael Schaper is the Deputy Chairman of the Australian Competition and Consumer Commission (ACCC), and has a special focus on small business, franchising, industry associations and business liaison.

A past president of the Small Enterprise Association of Australia and New Zealand, he brings extensive experience in the area of small business through his previous roles as Small Business Commissioner for the Australian Capital Territory ACT, a director of the International Council for Small Business and a manager of a community-based small business advisory centre. In 2009 the Council of Small Business Organisations of Australia named him 'National Small Business Champion'.

Dr Schaper is currently also an Adjunct Professor with Curtin University, a Senior Honorary Research Fellow with the University of Western Australia business school and chairs the advisory board of Griffith University's Asia-Pacific Centre for Franchising Excellence. He holds a PhD and a Master of Commerce degree from Curtin University, as well as a Bachelor of Arts from the University of Western Australia.

Dr Schaper is the author or co-author of numerous business management books and research papers, and sits on the board of several international SME journals. He is currently a member of the ACCC's Enforcement, Infrastructure and Adjudication committees.

My introduction to Michael was not through the normal channels and fortunately I was the one contacting him and not the other way around. Michael had accepted a speaking position at a conference I was hosting early in 2012. In comparison to all the other presenters

142

whose businesses and interests were directly aligned to the conference, he was there to try and educate the audience on the topic of collective bargaining (so as to avoid price colluding) and how small businesses could still work together to generate a mutual benefit without falling foul of the legislation. The topic is complex and often discussed with heated emotions by the audiences who were often uninformed and simply didn't understand the process. Michael presented effortlessly and made a very complex topic palatable. In fact his presentation received the highest score on the feedback results and generated the most amount of discussion.

From Michael's perspective.

> *I think as an organisation, we frame our customers first and foremost as the Australian public. We're a government agency and our role is to enforce the law on their behalf. There are secondary audiences that also come into play. The business community, for example, is very much one. There are sector specific audiences as well. We're one of those organisations that have a very wide range of different sectorial responsibilities. So there are many of them. That's from the organisation's point of view.*

Michael's viewpoint is clearly in line with the overall goals of the organisation and why wouldn't it be? He has been working for the ACCC for several years and holds a very senior position. However, on reflection he also noted that he has a secondary set of clients and stakeholders he needs to be responsible for, but his leadership role is quite different to the other leaders presented in this book. Michael explains that his internal clients, or stakeholders include: 'the staff that work up and report to you, the individuals you work with, and the people that you report up to. Ultimately, everyone answers to someone'.

Although this is not a new idea, Michael also has the secondary set of stakeholders, the Australian Government. 'Although the minister can't direct us, we still have to be mindful about what the government wants, what Parliament wants and about those stakeholders that still have an influence over the media'. The majority of private sector companies will have some form of shareholder group, either through a public or private style listing, but the ACCC is very different. We are defined as an independent Commonwealth statutory authority whose role is to enforce the *Competition and Consumer Act 2010* and a range of additional legislation, promoting competition, fair trading and regulating national infrastructure for the benefit of all Australians. While we are a statutory authority, which ultimately means we are independent from the government, we still have to operate within the legislative and judicial realms. That is, the Government will set the laws through its legislative powers and the judiciary will interpret them.

Michael defines his environment as 'an unusual management structure, where we have a seven-tier report. We have 700 staff and seven commissioners. Each commissioner has a section of the community they are responsible for. The teams that I work with most closely include those that are involved in small business issues, industry liaison and education and outreach. (The ACC receives) 80,000–90,000 customer and business complaints each year and we lack the resources to address each one. So there's a large amount of not only understanding the complaints but also respectfully saying to people, we're not going to be able to deal with this one for you. I know it matters to you for these reasons, but we can't take this any further. And that's not necessarily an easy one for people.'

While he works closely with those teams, he doesn't have the typical direct manager relationship; he supports the teams and provides guidance as well as some level of oversight. It is the guidance that often proves to be the most challenging. I posed the following question to Michael.

How do you motivate an individual when you don't have a direct line of sight of what their day-to-day job looks like? Or alternatively, if they are under a pile of paperwork and you've got this great new idea or process?

(For context – in your mind you're thinking, this is fantastic and they're looking at it and thinking, that's just another thing I have to do now.)

Michael answered quite prophetically, offering up three considerations that need to be called into play. 'I think it's a real issue. Before you run off with an idea, park it. If you're going to get angry, wait 24 hours before you respond. If you get enthused about something, give it 24 hours to see if you've still got the same enthusiasm. You need to be honest with yourself, to the extent that you can. Get some advice off your peers to see whether it sparks their interest before you go running to the staff'. Be respectful of your employees. Say to them, this is a suggestion; it's not a request. That means you need to frame it very carefully'. The simplicity and elegance of his sage advice is clearly a theme throughout this book – the simpler your approach; the more likely you are to have sustained success. Adding more complexity to your world may initially give a greater return, but in the long run you may end up tripping up yourself and the organisation. To ensure that Michael stays relevant in his organisation he is very aware of his position and the nuances of how he interacts with the staff.

The further you move up the hierarchy in any organisation, public or private, the less familiarity you have with the operational issues. Sometimes it is the operational issues that are terribly demotivating to the people on the ground. For example, it's all very well and good to talk about the big picture programs, but if the people you expect to do it are buried in paperwork, or the internal processes are so cumbersome that it's almost impossible for people to make decisions and do things, it can't be done. I'm not saying that that's the case here, but it's something you've got to be constantly aware of in your career as you move up the chain and you can often lose track of how easy or how hard it is for people on the ground and you can also lose track of what, in turn, motivates them. For many people who work in my area, in outreach and education, interaction with the public involves talking and explaining. It involves getting up in front of a group as much as it is about having a detailed knowledge and application of economics and law'.

It's always worth trying to spend some time making sure you can keep firmly on the ground. That being said, power and positions of power will always play a role and have an impact on the motivational culture of a business, I wonder when Richard Branson says, "I've got this really good idea" but you don't have to follow through on it, how many people in the Virgin empire say, "Yeah, we're not going to do that"'. Power in a statutory organisation takes on a completely different perspective and it's one that Michael is very aware of. 'You do have to be really careful of power and how it is both used and perceived." Michael explained how he would approach these situations, "If I'm going to try and foist something on the staff, having passed test number one (self-checking) and two (check in with the other ACCC Commissioners), I would then usually look at the senior bureaucratic levels. Hierarchy is one of the things that are really important, particularly in public service organisations. The chain of command is very valued and if you break that, you can create problems'. Michael explained how this concept of hierarchy often conflicts with egalitarianism, an approach that is considered very Australian. 'Egalitarianism works fine in a small business, and it can work fine in a not-for-profit, but there are lots of organisations that have a really good reason for having a bureaucracy'. He continued to suggest that even if a leader has good intentions and 'wants to be a motivator by showing a personal interest', the employee at the other end may be worrying, and questioning themselves.

As Michael sees it, this demonstrates that 'sometimes trying to be everyone's friend and trying to interact with them at that level creates more difficulty'.

I think we all need to pause here and reread this last statement. In my mind it captures eloquently the motivational mindset and in particular the motivation to avoid failure perfectly. Somehow our culture has created this shift and our role as leaders is to recognise this and start initiating the cure. If our society is going to flourish we need to instill and support the motivation to succeed mindset (MTS) and remove statements like the one presented above. The key factor in supporting a MTS mindset is the approach we take to failure. Michael, in his role as Deputy Chairman, has an added element which many other organisations are somewhat protected from: "the media". I am not suggesting that other organisations are not held to account by the media, but I would argue that in this instance the ACCC is held to a set of public standards, which are often determined by the individual and always driven by the context or environment they find themselves in. At your next dinner party bring up the topic of petrol pricing and collusion and watch the argument unveil. The ACCC, failure and the media can often be a volatile mix. Michael weighed in on the issue.

> *I think you often have to be careful in a workplace where you don't get judged by the 99 things that you did well, but the one thing that you did wrong. That's a real challenge if you're trying to motivate and manage people, because it actually causes people to keep their head down and be*

cautious. If you jump on people for the one thing they got wrong and fail to recognise the 99 things that they've done well, then you do create a culture where people retract and stay out of the firing range.

This mindset was once described to me by another senior member in a public sector as the CARE approach; "Cover Arse Retain Employment". The irony of the individual who shared that with me was that his department was charged with driving innovation and working on the third horizon (three to five years ahead). Needless to say, he has not been very successful in the role and has recently been moved into another position more suited to his management style. This approach simply couldn't work for Michael. He absolutely recognises that you need to make mistakes to, in his words, 'grow, learn, expand and push our limits. I guess the real test of that is when someone gets into a situation where something goes wrong'. Michael offered several motivational tools or strategies he uses with staff. 'Some of it can be incremental and involves taking little steps. There's a line I like to use with staff: "I trust your judgment". After having come to a point where you both figure out the options and you genuinely don't have a strong view, or if you think there are two or three good options, that line can be used. The follow up line is saying, "Whatever it is, I will stand by it"'. The second strategy is checking for understanding.

It is often easy to impart information and to say, 'I've given you all the tools, the background, the options, the pros and cons, what we can do, what we can't do, and the processes involved'. However sometimes it's really helpful to take a step back and ask the employee whether they know what it all means. Verbally ask them whether they actually understand, or if there is anything that needs recapping, which is an invitation to make sure they understand.

His final tool is checking for employee understanding and 'asking them to explain in their own words what you've just told them'.

After reflecting on Michael's strategies I have one more I would like to add for your consideration, and it comes in the form of a simple but very powerful statement any leader can make.

Now that we've explored the concept, tell me what you don't like.

This is very different from the statement of 'what do you think about this?' I appreciate the difference is semantic but the culture developed through the first question is far more inspirational than the second. Just consider which statement actually gives your staff permission to give their opinion.

In addition to supporting his teams internally, Michael also has a public facing role and is often called on to interact with the public. As mentioned early on in this chapter, the ACCC receives somewhere between 80,000–90,000 complaints every year, so one could easily imagine the type of mindset he sometimes faces. His approach to the public is one that is of a slightly different perspective.

'First of all there's assumed knowledge, which is the importance of always being familiar with the topic at hand'. The second level is acknowledging the knowledge that other people, particularly clients, also have.

> *You would assume that within your organisation, most of the people that you're dealing with are already committed to the big picture with regards to what you're trying to achieve as an organisation. However, you don't know your external audience. Industry groups are a classic example where you don't know what the politics are, either within, or sometimes between industry bodies and they can be quite strong. You can make blunders when you don't acknowledge what other people already know.*

Additionally, the third and final level involves the experiences of others:

> *I always seem to be surprised with just how much experience people have. No matter how old or young they are and no matter where they sit in the hierarchy compared to you, there's always someone who has experiences that I would never have dreamed of or that I would never see in my life. I remember helping someone start up a small business when I was running a small business centre in WA and at the very end he said, "The old guy that's retiring next to us, he used to be the Queen's private secretary". I never would have guessed that. You're always going to find your surprises out there.*

Michael's final message here is to do your homework. What may work for you internally may not always work externally. The major difference is the shift in power. While you may have some power you have lost the hierarchical power your organisation bestows upon you by default.

TAKE HOME

» Know all your stakeholders and don't forget the indirect ones who only have an influencing role; they can still be very powerful.

» 24 hours can save you. If you have it, use it.

» Peers will often bring a fresh set of eyes; make sure you encourage their input.

» Consider the framing of your statement.

» Recognise the disconnect between strategy and operational delivery. Actually use the tools your people are using to make sure they perform in the way you are expecting them to.

» Consider the one element that will negate all the good work you have done and plan for it.

» Your presence can be very powerful. Understand it and use it effectively.

BEN LAWRENCE
Head of HR – Wesfarmers

Ben Lawrence was appointed Chief Human Resources Officer for Wesfarmers Limited in February 2008.

Prior to joining Wesfarmers, Ben was the global head of Human Resources for Foster's Group Limited based in Melbourne, Australia from 2001. Prior to Foster's, Ben held a variety of senior executive roles in the United States including Chief Human Resources Officer with Beringer Wine Estates, Vice President International Human Resources with the Clorox Company, a global consumer goods company, and Human Resources Director with FMC Company, a global diversified mining, minerals and chemicals business.

Ben is currently a non-executive director of two non-profit organisations: Red Dust, focused on indigenous health and wellness; and the Wunan Foundation, focused on improving Aboriginal education, employment and accommodation in the East Kimberley region. He holds a Bachelor of Science in Business / Labour Relations from Utah State University and advanced management education from the University of Pennsylvania and the University of Michigan.

I will always remember how Ben and I first me. He greeted me at the Wesfarmers Melbourne office with a very firm handshake and a question, which was followed by another question, and another and concluded with the question, 'how can I help you, what doors can I open?' After getting to know Ben I questioned him on this approach and he commented to me that he views himself as a concierge. His job is to understand the situation and try to open the most appropriate doors – hence all the questions.

Wesfarmers, a conglomerate based in Perth, Australia employs about

200,000 across the globe. The Wesfarmer model is portfolio based with only about 200 employees employed at head office. This corporate structure is very different to many others but clearly works for them. The group in 2014 generated over $62 billion dollars returning a net profit of $1.6 billion.

Ben defines the Wesfarmers' approach as 'We set the tone and have a governance model; we are simply portfolio managers'. Each company within the model is directed by its own CEO and they (Wesfarmers) play an oversight role. Within this role is the challenging task of ensuring the best people are steering the ship. 'What is important is that we get the right MD in place who is motivated to drive their particular business – but still recognises that we need to ultimately drive shareholder value. Our main driver in the Wesfarmers group office is how do we create value for our shareholders? It is a singular focus but highly complex in the levers that enable it. The characteristic we look for in an MD is that they think holistically around their particular business'.

Wesfarmers has an eclectic group of companies ranging from retail, chemical, fertilisers, industrial and mining, and therefore a 'one size fits all' strategy will not always work. 'We are always conscious that we need to provide a satisfactory return on every particular investment, which, as you can imagine is sometimes challenging as ROI (return on investment) is not an exact science nor is everyone expecting the same return'. Therefore Ben is focused on understanding what gets them up in the morning and what is going to drive them to deliver the expected ROI within the specific context of their business model.

The next challenge facing Ben is how to create a fair and equitable reward system. 'We need to ensure we pay them a fair wage, which is in itself an interesting and complicated factor, as how do you define fair? In most cases it is internal equity – "I am being paid a fair amount for what I contribute to the organisation as a whole and compared to others."

It is a simple economic supply and demand model. Once that has been resolved, it falls back to the motivation of the individual. What I have found interesting is that in most cases it is the control over their own destiny, which drives and motivates them. Real ownership around their business, coupled with the appropriate authority is essential. They need to be able to make decisions and then live and die by them'.

Wesfarmers doesn't have a matrix management, each executive team owns their line of business and is held accountable for the delivery of their strategic plans. They control the resources which ultimately drives the outcomes and that is essential. 'We don't have a significant amount of finger pointing around here; we have removed the blame model which is often seen in other organisations. All too often we hear, "I would be able to achieve X and Y if I was only given tool A and investment B". Wesfarmers has removed this barrier, we have removed the excuses. That is not to say it doesn't have its drawbacks, but these are often the uncontrollable. We can't control the economy; we can only react to it. We can't control the weather patterns, but we can have some systems in place to react should the worst case present itself.'

While many organisations may look the same on the surface, when you consider their purpose, the people and the drivers within the business can be very different and that takes a different mindset to drive. Coles, their largest retailer has around 100,000 employees and is dispersed across Australia, while Bunnings has around 30,000 and is also Australia wide. Overtly they are both entities that sell products, but the nature of the product and the expectations of their customers can be very different. They have had many executives join us from other organisations and the issue of accountability and authority is always raised. 'In most instances all our lateral hires have experienced the accountability model in which they have the authority to say no. Granted this essential, our model provides them with the authority to say yes. We have really worked hard at trying to break down the bureaucracy'.

When you boil it down, it becomes very interesting as we are dealing with humans and they are in nothing unpredictable. We recognise that work is only one part of your life – albeit an important one, but if we don't recognise the person as a whole we often don't engage well enough to gain their discretionary effort. If all we ever do is consider work as an isolated component, then the outcome will follow that line of thinking and the effort displayed will be commensurate. Ben recognises that 'the individual who comes to work brings both their head and their heart and both are just as important, but how do we capture both. The answer is simple as it is complex and it starts with the quality of the workplace'. For Ben this is made up of several variables. 'The people I am working with, the content of the job, the culture of the environment and finally the respect of their manager'.

We know from the literature that people will stay in a role that they dislike longer if they like the people they are working with, as opposed to a role they enjoy but working with people they dislike.

So how do you build that culture? Well it does start with the base level pay, which as discussed earlier needs to be fair, but after that it is the 'hygiene factors', which come into play. Ben recalled a lecture given by a professor very early on in his career, on how pay affects culture.

Pay is a pretty powerful motivator, but once it has hit your pocket it loses all its power. Pay actually has no impact on motivation, which is what is required for you to continue to work. As long as you do an OK job you will continue to get paid, but clearly this won't affect your discretionary effort.

So as you move up, pay simply has to satisfy the fair test and answer the question 'Am I being treated fairly amongst my peers and in relation to my work effort?' But after that they become more interested in the company's investment in them as a whole person. Here is where we move into the continual development angle, where individuals are more interested in being developed than paid more.

Questions Ben often hears are:

Does my boss receive the same development?
Am I being mentored and coached?
Is this a safe working environment?
Does my company care and give back to the community

These and many other aspects form the motivational component of productivity and can be significantly impacted on an organisation. The sense of accomplishment is paramount.

The concept of community support requires some more fleshing out as over the years it appears to have altered somewhat, and the expectations of the individual has altered. Historically speaking, companies would often align with a specific organisation and provide them with either direct injection of funds or in-kind support through resource sharing or hands and feet. This was successful however, many organisations have started to change their viewpoint, as aligning to one company limited your impact on the entire community and also limited the impact you may have had on staff if they didn't align to that group.

'What we are seeing of late is a shift into a version of the technology BYOD (Bring Your Own Device) concept whereby the individual can ultimately choose the way they want the company to spend its community dollar. Nowadays we try where possible to allow individuals to choose where they spend their community time but do it on our time! The net benefit is huge, the company benefits from an expanded community program and the individual feels like they have made a difference (and we have supported that). Win-win all round'.

Once we build the inspiration people will take it a point far beyond anything you could ever imagine.

Team vs. Individual

All the above refers to the individual and what they require to be motivated at work and provide a level of discretionary effort. But like a sporting team, there is not only individual motivation but also team motivation. Team motivation is different and is characterised by the team being successful, even if the individual fails to meet their own goals. This environment brings a whole set of additional challenges. The difference in this mindset is the concept of winning. Winning as a team can often override the need for the individual to win and also allows for individuals with complementary skills to work well together.

> *'I often look to the feedback I receive from 360 degree evaluation but also from other factors like the desire to join my team, as well as turnover rates. The current data suggests I am doing an OK job (humility is definitely a factor) but the lesson learned here and one that I like to pass onto other managers is that you don't have many tools at your discretion to motivate your staff. Pay is usually set by the organisation (you may have some latitude but it is usually limited), but what you can control is job content and how people work together to achieve a desired outcome. What the team does and what they find meaning in, will keep them coming back to work and not only work for themselves but also work for the team'.*

Another factor for Ben is the physical environment people operate in.

'We are all wedded to this concept of an office, but what if we removed those constraints and provided people the opportunity to work in an environment that is conducive to their needs? The likely outcome is one of enhanced productivity. Flexibility is something you can absolutely control, it may be as simple as letting people come to work in clothing of their choice or leaving at a particular time to watch their kids play sport. Remember we are dealing with adults and we need to maintain that perspective'.

If we micro manage and take away any form of personal control and decision making from them, we are going to have significant trouble getting the team to gel (to use a sporting analogy). 'I need to give them the canvas and the tools and then just let them know the style of painting I need. Be careful not to be too lax in your control or the contemporary painting you wanted will end up being water lilies. But I think you get the message.'

I appreciate that there is a major BUT in that approach and there will always be people who choose to take advantage of a situation. We as leaders should not let this be the reason not to do something, but in fact the way we handle people who don't play by the rules can in and of itself highlight the type of culture you are looking to create.

Managing poor performers is essential and vital to a high performing culture. In this capacity the more important element is time and fairness–responding in real time and within a degree of fairness (viewed by others as a measured and appropriate response) is essential.

But is it different with the CEO's and senior executives of your organisations, do they respond in different ways?

While the above all does hold true at the higher level, there is one factor we do need to explore and it's often one that is viewed negatively by society but quite frankly is essential and useful when used appropriately. That factor is EGO.

Ben took his time to respond and was quite thoughtful is his words. 'I would love to say that power and access are not factors but in truth they are. The desire for power is not as demonstrated by the evil villain from any bad B grade movie and usually doesn't require you to have a special look while raising your pinkie finger to the side of your mouth, (if you are unsure of what I am referring to head over to Google and search for Dr. Evil and a million dollars). Power and control plays a role but only to serve as an internal motivator for the individual (if desired by the individual). Power when used as an external motivator will often see a short term gain, but have a long term negative impact on the culture. Successful leaders recognise this and use it sparingly.. The other aspect that definitely comes into play is that of reputation. Individuals who aspire to reach the very top will protect their reputation with every last fibre of their being. It is the one factor, which enables them not only to become successful but also to remain successful. We can all think of high flying CEO's and executives who have not protected their reputation, or whose behaviour has clearly redefined the way we view them. Those individuals don't usually last very long in their roles and when they do move it's often a move into obscurity. Protecting your reputation becomes a very powerful internal motivator and one, which, thankfully is aligned to the motivation to succeed mindset. By effectively considering all the pre-mentioned variables you will enable an individual to protect their reputation, deliver a return to the shareholder, still have their people wanting to work for them and arguably most importantly, leave behind a legacy you can be proud of. If you are going to invest vast amounts of time along with personal sacrifice that is usually experienced firsthand by your family, you want to know that it was worth it'.

Think about the current Wesfarmers' story, Michael Chaney (the previous CEO) handed it to Richard Goyder the current CEO, who will hand to the next person in due course what is in effect a 100 year old success story. The question Richard will have to answer is what type of a company he will hand over? The leaders are simply the shepherds of the entity and it will always be bigger than them, so what mark will they leave on the flock? How will they impact on the DNA of the organisation and can I ensure that it is in a better position now than when they received it.

There will be some who may reflect on the turnaround at Coles, which began in 2008 in which several new executives were brought in with significant bonuses attached to their salaries, designed to remunerate them on achieving a pre-determined return on the $20 billion dollar investment that was made. Ben recognised that the monetary return was fantastic but 'the reputational and legacy drivers were far more entrenched and significant'. Ben argues that they were just as likely to work that hard if they weren't receiving the additional bonuses. 'While the money was nice, the bigger picture here is that they were handed a broken asset and left it being a world-class retailer. Consider their resumes, they won't say "I made x many dollars" they will say, "I turned around Coles". The reality is that Coles had all but been written off and was likely to fall into foreign hands. While not everything has been perfect, today it's a switched on organisation that its team members can be proud of. Hard one to prove but it is in line with the executive insight provided before; I guess it's up to you to decide?'

After all the discussions with Ben around CEO's and the legacies they leave behind, I am reminded of a comment I once heard made by the CEO of a large organisation during a speech he gave at a networking function which explored the answer he gave to his children as to why he couldn't spend more time with them. His answer was that he was responsible for ensuring that 55,000 other families could spend time together stress free and with food on the table. While he appreciated that his kids didn't really care for the answer (and who would blame them) he, the CEO personally took some solace from the greater good.

TAKE HOME

» Fairness is as important at the executive level as it is throughout the organisation and it needs to be linked to the value of the business.

» Managers need to consider the level of flexibility they actually have.

» Consider the levers needed to say yes, don't just give people permission to say no.

» Comfort is king. If your people need their special security blankets at work, let them bring them. 'Bring your own device' technology is already here, ignore it at your peril.

» An office doesn't make a company, the people do. Consider how flexible your company can be in its working arrangement

» Understand ego and power exist in an organisation regardless of how much you may try to remove it. Don't ignore it.

GORDON LEFEVRE
Chief Financial Officer – AMP

Mr. Gordon J. Lefevre has been Chief Financial Officer at AMP Limited since March 1, 2014. He maintains a number of other key external relationships including those with the ATO, Group Auditors and major suppliers. Over a 13-year period he served as Deputy Group Chief Financial Officer of National Australia Bank Limited and prior was the General Manager of Personal Financial Services Australia for NAB. He served as an Executive Vice president of Homeside Lending Inc. He joined Homeside in September 2001 serving as Chief Financial Officer until November 14, 2001. Gordon has over 18 years of international financial experience. He began his career in 1983 at Deloitte, Haskins and Sells.

In 1987, he joined First National Bank of South Africa, where he served a Senior Manager. In 1990, he moved to Melbourne, Australia as a Senior Manager at KPMG. Gordon joined National Australia Bank, Melbourne, Australia in 1995 as a senior member of the Bank's acquisition team. In 2000, he relocated to Glasgow, Scotland and served as General Manager of Finance and Strategy for National Australia Group Europe Limited. He served as Chief Financial Officer at Grocon Pty Ltd., and was responsible for the Grocon Group's finance and information technology functions. He has been the Chairman of AMP Group Finance Services Limited since August 27, 2014 and has been its Director since March 1, 2014. Gordon has a Bachelor of Accounting Science (Honours) from the University of South Africa, a Bachelor of Commerce from the University of Kwazulu-Natal, South Africa and is a Chartered Accountant.

It was a Thursday morning around 9 am when I slowly walked up to a

162

man that was sitting at his desk, simultaneously looking at his iPad and his computer screen. He noticed me out of the corner of his eye, peered up from his desk, knowing perfectly well why I was approaching him and said, 'you're early, the crisis simulation is not due to start till 9.30 am!' My response was [apologetically] that I was sorry, but when a crisis hits it doesn't do so on a schedule. We were about to run a 90-minute crisis exercise with the entire senior executive team...

The man, Craig Meller the CEO of AMP looked over the inject (a written hypothetical scenario) in his hand which suggested a major cyber-attack was occurring in his organisation. Twitter was metaphorically on fire and the fake media was likely to be on his door within minutes. He calmly called his EA over and asked her to contact Gordon and get him to the crisis room ASAP. Once he knew Gordon was en-route, he called his other direct reports and asked them to make their way to the crisis room. As I walked in the room I noticed Gordon sitting in the chair's position, he had already made the space his; his computer and note pad were set up how he wanted it, he had the projector screen up and running and as more people entered the room he simply took over. For the next hour Gordon led the crisis team through a variety of simulated scenarios, which were designed to test their emotional and cognitive resolve and ensure that he and his team were competent and confident to guide the 10,000 or so AMP staff members should a real crisis actually occur.

Over the past year I have developed a tool, which enables me to measure and evaluate an individual's ability to perform consistently under pressure. The output of the tool is a heat map that indicates the level of emotional, decision making and behavioural responses an individual has to each. Gordon has given me permission to share his profile tool, which is quite frankly exemplary.

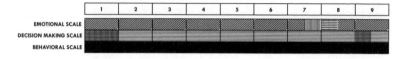

Each number on the table represents a unique inject. Injects are simulated situations or actions which could occur in the business, designed to stress test the crisis teams decision making and ensure their crisis plan was suitable. What you are seeing is an individual who remained calm regardless of the situation that was presented to him. His decision making style was almost perfectly proactive and he anticipated a number of the challenges headed his way. Under pressure he remained engaged throughout the simulation. The key above indicates the responses that Gordon demonstrated, but does not paint the full picture. The additional emotional variables I often observe in others include: nervousness, anger, frustration and despair. While the behavioural variables include the desire to flee or the inability to act at all. As the pressure built up and it did (we even had the actual Chair of Board make a simulated call into the CEO for a briefing) Gordon didn't break stride. Within the created scenario Gordon was required to suggest or infer the actions that he and the team would take. However, just a few months prior to the simulation, he was in the same chair guiding his organisation through the Martin Place siege. His role on that day as he has described it to me was no different from how he handled the simulation, although he was the first to suggest that he is brutal when it comes to continual development. While he handled the situation similarly, he had made a number of subtle changes to his current approach which he now felt enabled him to be more effective in the role.

This approach to crisis management appears to be no different to his approach to motivation and how he interacts with his organisation. 'The first thing you have to do is to take your job seriously but not take yourself seriously and if you unpick that, what is that all about? That's all about, for my part, being human. Showing humility and being authentic are paramount. If you're going to motivate somebody you've got to be authentic'. We often hear the concept of authenticity but I have always wondered what exactly that means. Like the motivational mindset, which unfortunately acts independent of society and is wholly aligned to the individual, authenticity appears to do the same. The dictionary defines authenticity as concerning the truthfulness of origins, attributes, commitments, sincerity, devotion, and intentions. The definition is clear but it does exactly define the mindset, which is determining each of those variables. I questioned Gordon as to the definition he uses and his response has fitted the overall theme of this book, simply and elegantly. 'Be true to yourself. I do think that that's only the beginning because the other thing that you have to be able to do, is to be absolutely crystal clear with them about what it is that you expect and also have a dialogue with them about their interpretation of the situation because if you just say this is what I want you to do, that's not communication, because what do they hear? So let them play back to you'.

Gaining clarity in the message is only really the first part and it satisfies the cognitive and logical part of the brain effectively. At this point, the emotional brain is still left wanting. We all might agree on the communication but there is still another step. 'Once you've got this really established foundation of clarity and then you have to for my part, back away to let them work. Empower them, but also to let them know that they are supported and you will back them 100 per cent, without this doubt may set in'. Doubt is a powerful emotion, it creeps up on you when you least expect it and then before you know it, it has taken over every aspect of your thoughts and behaviours. We don't know what causes doubt but acknowledge it probably resides in our emotional brain. We often describe it as a feeling but with very powerful associated thoughts. "I'm not sure I can do this" – seven very powerful words that have been the start of many an undoing. In many cases the cause of doubt is due to a failure to recognise the skill set you already have to negotiate the course – consider the example of a professional athlete in the finals who simply forgets how to throw or kick a ball. Gordon was well aware of this process and has a strategy in tow.

> *In having the dialogue with them around that clarity, asking 'do they have the skills in order to execute on what it is that you want them to do?' and 'do they also have the self-belief?' Sometimes they need to be given a little bit of a reminder about how good they are, or that they have some potential that's unrealised. They need to feel supported in their challenge but at the same time you need to back away so they can have a real crack at it. They need to be truly empowered.*

The downside of this approach is that it requires significantly more effort on the part of the leaders – but as Gordon puts it, 'motivation is not about telling somebody what it is that you want done and then setting a task that is incredibly stretching. That may slightly motivate some. Certainly not going to motivate all. For me, motivation is about creating a climate that allows everyone to succeed, but it's not just about your stars, but also those people who are average performers. If you can motivate an average performer to achieve way above and beyond what they ordinarily do, you place yourself in a fantastic position to really help someone achieve their full potential'. Interestingly, Gordon uses the word motivation, yet in the context of the discussion and the motivational mindset, he is far from motivating. His approach would be far better described as inspirational and one that relies on his actions speaking far louder than his words. 'There's this issue of role modelling. We have known for years that money is not as powerful a motivator as we initially thought, what will motivate people is looking at leaders and seeing whether what they say is also what they do. We need to all step up!"

Every leader approaches their direct staff in a particular way, which is often informed by their experience, emotional intelligence and overall attitude to leadership. This interaction is one that is very much controllable as they are able to receive direct and indirect feedback as to how successful the interaction is. The greater challenge is interacting and influencing individuals who do not directly report to you. Gordon recognises the challenge but overcomes it with a simple strategy "Be interested in them". You may be quite surprised how many conversations you will have with people throughout your week / year who do not directly report to you, but you still have an influence over, Gordon maintained that you 'must always BE in the conversation. For that moment in time when you are conversing with someone, they need to know and feel that you are interested in them'. Gordon has implemented a strategy called a skip meeting. A skip meeting or sometimes referred to as a 'manager-once-removed' meeting, is a meeting you as a leader have with your direct reports, direct reports. The goal of the meeting is not to check in on their boss or how they are performing in their current role, but to actually understand who they are and what their career aspirations are (i.e. what motivates them). 'I've had lots of wonderful fortunate experiences as a leader, to do these skip meetings, where when you're sitting with a person not as their boss but as an interested party wanting to understand what they do. People come away so motivated'.

Gordon had some additional advice should you wish to implement a skip meeting program.

» Don't tell them what to do. You never tell them what to do.
» Always ask about what they do.
» Ask about what their challenges are.
» Show authentic and genuine interest.
» Offer some observations.

But you don't always get a chance to have these types of meetings and you need to consider alternative strategies to expand your influence. Gordon reflected on a strategy and a lesson he learnt after taking over the running of Personal Financial Services for NAB. 'I would make the point of travelling as often as I could to a branch or a series of branches that housed our personal/relationship bankers and financial planners. I would always ensure that I meet with the branch manager to understand the idiosyncrasies of that branch (you never want to assume they were all the same)'. To further enhance his insights of the team, Gordon added 'once a quarter I would be a teller for a day, so that when I sat down and talked with the staff, I could talk on empathetically about what was going on in their branch'. Gordon was always never surprised by the great insights the staff had. 'They live and breathe the job everyday, we in leadership roles just need to listen more'.

He reflected on one particular meeting that occurred shortly after a branch had been robbed. 'Robberies in branches are particularly gut wrenching. My security people taught me early on that every robbery is pre-meditated. They're quite brutal things, as most are pre-meditated crimes. You don't just wander in off the street and rob a bank. They spend time thinking about which branch to rob and why. They case the joint, effectively spying on the staff. It's not pretty; it's often very violent. Hence, when it happens, everyone in the branch feels violated. So you have to approach these people and these situations very sensitively'. He continued to emphasise that he had never been in that type of situation so could only imagine how they would be feeling and therefore spent many hours contemplating how to best support his staff who had.

Gordon reflected on a particular robbery, and as soon as he heard about what happened he made his way to the bank to simply let them know he cared. 'I could have called and said, "I'm sorry and I'm thinking about you" but that is not being authentic. That's just doing what the manual says you should do'. Gordon wanted to look them in the eye and say, 'I'm sorry you were robbed today it must be a dreadful experience and I can only imagine as a human being what you're going through, I want you to know that I am here to listen to you'. For him 'it's got to be authentic. You can't use a script. They will smell bullshit a mile away'.

I was surprised to hear that on average his bank would experience a robbery once a month. On every occasion, in addition to visiting the bank (if possible) he would always make a point of writing a personal note to the branch manager saying he was aware of the robbery and interested in the wellbeing of each and every staff member, he would also offer them his personal help if they needed it. Sure, he reflected on his experience of being a teller for a day each quarter but he had never been robbed. In an awful twist of fate, one bank in which he had been a teller for a day, was subsequently robbed a couple of months later. The phone call from Gordon to the manager had a profound impact on the team as well as himself. 'I knew everyone in that branch by name and I was mostly concerned about this team of people who I had the chance to meet and get to know. Putting a name to the face really makes it real and my heart really went out to them'. Gordon reflected on this being one of his most challenging and difficult times in his career.

To be able to operate as a leader like this, you can't simply pick the best moments to demonstrate your leadership. The Clayton leader who shows up to save the day but is not prepared to put in the hard years will ultimately never gain the respect of their teams. Gordon suggested that as quickly as he would attend a robbery or some other crisis-like event, he was just as likely to 'drop down into finance and go and sit with somebody. I knew enough about what they're doing to show a genuine interest. I recall seeing a very frustrated individual once who was completing a year end reconciliation, I asked why they were looking frustrated and he must have felt very comfortable with me as he informed me just how upset he was due to the change which was occurring which included several redundancies'. Gordon could have played the party line and simply referred him to his line manager to discuss his concerns but he didn't. Instead he maintained the same level of authenticity he has referred to throughout this chapter. 'We spoke openly and honestly, I said, "Yes there've been some staff cuts, it'll be tough to see some of your colleagues leave, do you know why we're doing it?"' Gordon went on to explain the reasons but never apologised for the strategy, instead he had this wonderful piece of wisdom: 'Don't dumb it down and don't, for god's sake, ever, ever, ever be condescending to people, treat them as if they are absolutely one of a kind'.

The impact of your ability to create a motivating environment is often greater than what you think and your team and others in the organisation will infer your intentions not just by what you say but also by what you do.

Gordon posed a question, which I challenge you to answer.

What shadow do you cast as a leader? Are you authentic and consistent?

This level of self- awareness is apparent in every interaction that I have had with Gordon and no more so than in his description of a challenging situation he found himself in several years earlier. In a similar vein to the section with Giam Sweigers the CEO of Aurecon, in which Giam discussed the values of his company and then highlighted the similarities the words had to Enron, a company that clearly didn't live up to those values. Gordon had joined a company after completing a significant amount of due diligence into their values as well as those of the leadership team. All was progressing incredibly well until the company faced an extremely challenging situation surrounding a safety issue. The physical situation was clearly out of the control of the leadership team and they were discussing how to respond.

Gordon reflects a single comment that changed forever his perceptions of where true north was on that company's moral compass; The statement: 'if you're in this business long enough, this is going to happen'. Gordon described how this was counter to many espoused values for that company and hence he made a decision on the spot that the values of the company did not reflect his own and he was not happy casting a leadership shadow there anymore. The biggest issue for Gordon was that he sincerely didn't believe that this mindset extended beyond the individual who made it, in fact, he argued that 'what I saw from the response teams was incredibly genuine and that was actually throughout the organisation, the way that people operated the day of and during the night of that incident was exemplary. If the people on the front line had heard a comment like that from any senior leader in the company, I'm not sure they would be putting in the discretionary effort or perhaps showing the company the kind of loyalty they all blindly did'.

What happened next for Gordon was, in his own words, 'deeply principle led'. He immediately handed in his letter of resignation. A number of different conversations were had as he exited the organisation, including one about a minor issue of a bonus owing to him. In the whole scheme of things it was minor but it became a matter of principle when he was informed he would not be receiving it. 'I went to my son's speech night and the head of school, a young lady was talking about what the school did for her was that it enabled her to find her voice. It was such a gutsy little performance on the stage, for somebody who had obviously grown over the year from a somewhat more timid young lady. I went home that night and I wrote this stinging note using my newly found voice'. While everything was resolved, Gordon's reflection from the entire incident was solely focused on the lesson he learnt from the school captain who spoke that night. 'I got my inspiration for this from a young lady who stood up and said she found her voice. I found mine and have never lost it since'.

We never really know where our inspiration comes from and it is difficult to often recreate it on the spot but when it happens it can last a lifetime. Gordon may have received motivating commentary by those around him and much of it would have been very sound sage advice, but he didn't shift on the continuum until that speech. What is more amazing is that unless she reads this book and puts two and two together she is unlikely to ever know the impact she had. The message here is perfectly in line with Gordon's viewpoint on the shadow you cast. You may never know the impact you have on people as the actions often occur out of context and within their time line not yours. So be careful how you cast that shadow and never let your age or tenure in a business deter you.

Gordon left me with his final views on motivating as a leader.

If you look at leadership per se, it is about being out the front. It is a lonely place, it is a dangerous place at times and the world doesn't really have that many good leaders because of that factor. I do think that motivating is about flex. What I mean by that, is you have to make the judgment in real time, that sometimes mean motivating from the front and sometimes motivating from behind, but being able to know the difference between inspiration and motivation is the key. The shift needs to be innate, thinking I'm going to go into inspirational mode now, or I'm going to go into motivational mode reduces your authenticity. I think good leaders are those who can flex, who can stand in front of a group of people and authentically simplify things down and provide the right mix of motivation and inspiration.

To achieve this outcome we as leaders need to continue placing ourselves in a variety of situations and considering our responses. We furthermore need to continually evaluate and debrief our leadership decisions with a continual development mindset. The further we get from the coalface of the business the greater the need to reality check our leadership decisions.

Throughout the interview with Gordon, I was recalling an encounter with very senior solicitor several years earlier, his situation was not unique, but was a first for him. About 20 years earlier the solicitor was asked to make a member of his staff redundant. Being his first time, he decided to rip the band-aid off and get it done quickly, so he delivered the bad news in the best way possible. While he didn't recall exactly what he said, he vividly recalled the reaction of the individual who left the room sobbing. He was disappointed in this reaction as he felt he had been very professional and expected the person to take it on the chin. Without having anyone at work to discuss it with (it wasn't really part of the culture then) he went home and discussed it with his wife. Her response was simple and elegant, 'let me tell you why she ended up sobbing you #$%^'. After that incident he was determined to never find himself in that position again and here he was some 20 years later sharing with his colleagues his strategy of firing, promoting, interviewing, reviewing his wife once a month as a form of rehearsal. He claimed he would test his approach with her in a variety of situations and gain honest and transparent feedback. He proudly stated, 'it didn't take me very long to change and I feel like I am better leader now than I would have ever been without my wife's assistance'.

The question you should be considering now is, who is going to help you?

TAKE HOME

» Take your job seriously, just not yourself.

» Reminding someone of their potential can be very powerful.

» Spend time in the business making connections, when issues present always front them face-to-face.

» Be legitimately interested in your people – consider using skip meetings to enhance your understanding.

» Get on road; go on a listening tours frequently.

» People will smell bullshit a mile away, so just leave it at home.

» Don't be afraid to find inspiration outside your normal environment.

» Consider who will give you the honest and transparent feedback you need to develop.

PROF CARLOS SCHIENKESTEL
Head of Alfred Hospital Intensive care unit (ICU)

Prof Carlos Scheinkestel, MB BS, FRACP, Dip DHM, FCICM is the Director of the Department of Intensive Care and Hyperbaric Medicine at the Alfred Hospital. He is a physician who has been practising full time in intensive care since 1987 and was a Foundation member of the Joint Faculty of Intensive Care Medicine and now the College of Intensive Care Medicine. He was the Chairman of the Victorian Branch and a member of the Board of Directors of the Australian and New Zealand Intensive Care Society (ANZICS) from 1998 to 2002. In 2000, he was appointed by the Department of Human Services (Victoria) to the Ministerial Emergency and Critical Care Committee and in 2009 to the Intensive Care Advisory Committee. Currently he holds a number of roles in key Hospital Committees.

He has a number of publications, and has given many invited presentations, both within Australia and overseas. His major interests are varied and include haemofiltration, renal failure, nutrition in the critically ill and leadership.

Sometimes you just get it right. I am a huge fan of the supposed overnight success, especially when you realise it has actually taken several years of hard work to make it look this easy. Imagine a world of professionals who have unilaterally made a decision to work for the greater good of the group. Let me expand. This imaginary world is made up of incredible well-educated professionals who are deemed, if not the best of the best, incredibly close. They could all run a private practice and generate significant additional revenue for themselves and they don't. In fact, they choose to work as a collaborative, in which all of the private practice earnings are collated in a pool of funds and then allocated back to the department for such things as the purchase of new equipment for the entire group. The rest of the revenue is then shared equally among the members. What would you say if this imaginary situation were actually true and operating (yes pun intended) within the highly specialised intensive care unit at the Alfred Hospital? Prof Carlos Scheinkestel leads an amazing group of specialists who not only run the highly awarded ICU at the Alfred, but they also run a well-oiled private practice. The practice provides the team members with additional equipment and services that enables the ICU to remain at the leading edge, and returns the additional revenue to them in equal shares (regardless of effort – that being said non-contributing members would simply not last in this highly motivated environment).

Back to Carlos. While the majority of the other contributors to this book were able to not only converse with their teams but also communicate directly with their clients to ascertain their needs and understand their concerns, this is not as easy for Carlos. 'Most of my patients are on life support. You can't have conversations with them. There are times when we have the ability to have a chat, often it may be a serious and important conversation, but most of the time, they either come to us after some catastrophic event or from the operating theatre and are unable to communicate with us. It's not an area where there are lots of interactions with patients. Lots with relatives, but not so much with patients'. Carlos' world is very different from that of corporate Australia, although he has the same issues regarding budgets and personnel as everyone else. From his perspective the Alfred is, at 45 beds, one of the largest Intensive Care Units in Australia. 'We admit about 3,000 patients a year. More than half of our workload is in state services. We do all of the artificial hearts for Victoria, South Australia, and Tasmania. We do the heart and lung transplants for those three areas. We do the pediatric lung transplants for all of Australia. We are the Victorian adult burns centre, and the hyperbaric centre for Victoria. We are one of two State adult trauma centres, and one of the largest in the country. We are one of two Victorian HIV centres, and one of two Victorian bone marrow transplant centres'.

A large amount of Carlos' intensive care unit work is therefore state service and high-end type work. 'We admit more patients between 6 pm and 6 am than between 6 am and 6 pm. On weekends, we exchange elective surgery for emergency trauma, so we basically run the same whether it's daytime, nighttime, weekday or weekend. It makes no difference to us'. To cope with this, he has a team of '21 specialists and 44 doctors in various stages of training, over 400 nursing staff, and about 20–30 support staff'. Compared to many other organisations this state of the art facility is managed on an extremely conservative budget of about '$55 million in total'.

With all of this going on, Carlos has a very simple definition of his role. 'My role is to make sure that the department runs perfectly and smoothly. It has the potential to be a major choke point if it doesn't'. Why? 'We have almost 10 per cent of the beds in the hospital, and in an organisation dealing with the case-mix we do, an inefficient ICU has the ability to really impede patient flow through the organisation. There are also huge financial impacts to the organisation if we don't run smoothly'. But in all of this, his biggest challenge is not the grieving relatives or the unconscious complex clients, it's not different from the bulk of leaders out there, it is "People Management". Fortunately for Carlos he recognised this issue very early on in his appointment and has systematically created an environment designed to mitigate and reduce risk, whilst encouraging good behaviour and performance. Carlos inherited his team in 2005 and admits that at the beginning it was tough. 'It's hard and you've got to start with what you've got. The potential was there though and I'm actually quite fortunate because I'm now 10 years down the track in this job, and I've now got this incredibly motivated, high-performing group of specialists that have evolved into a great team'.

Cognisant of the fact that the team still had to deliver medical services to an ever-growing number of patients, Carlos still spent a significant amount of time understanding and working with them. 'We spent a lot of time developing the team. When I first started, one of the first things we did was craft a mission statement. It sounds really corny, but we all got together, and sat around for weeks and argued over every single word. Ten years down the track, there is not a single word I would change'. It is where everyone wanted the department to be going forward.

He explained further, 'We started off with the concept that what's good today is not going to be good enough for tomorrow. We have to constantly improve and develop, keep getting better and better. So we talked about continuous improvement, the barriers to improvement, and then we set about on a process to try to make this easier to achieve'. Organisational change psychologists were engaged to assist the process.

This process began by using a form of personality testing, the Myers Briggs, which measures psychological preferences in how people perceive the world and make decisions and categorises people according to 16 personality types. 'All the Intensive Care specialists completed Myers Briggs profiles. The spread was almost across the entire grid. We then spent a year understanding how the different personality types communicate and improving our communication techniques. Next, we undertook an assessment of the Intensivists' behavioural strengths and weaknesses in the workplace, using the Belbin Team Roles Instrument. A team role is defined as a tendency to behave, contribute and interrelate with others in a particular way. Different individuals display different team roles to varying degrees. For example, every team has got members with bright ideas but who often struggle to get them anywhere and members that excel at implementation but don't necessarily have their own ideas. Using Belbin Team roles, everybody more clearly understood their strengths and role in the group. We got rid of offices, except for the directors, and everyone went into rooms with multi-work stations, and the productivity of the group went through the roof. They all talk to each other and bounce ideas off each other. For instance, the guy that's a great implementer is with the guy that has great ideas, so one comes up with the idea and the other helps take it somewhere'.

While many leaders would embark on such a rigorous endeavour, most would get to the end of pre-determined period and think, 'okay we're done with that' and move on. Carlos has taken the opposite view and continues to this day bringing the team together on a regular basis to continue the conversation. 'Each year we would recap on the year gone and then consider a new theme. After nine years of this, the group is really far advanced now. In the last year or so we've brought along a range of new concepts. Some are business concepts, such as, you have to be unique, add value, and be difficult to imitate. The group keeps on coming up with new initiatives and new challenges and just keep on getting better'.

Another innovation is how the team uses the revenue generated from their private practice.

> *As a group, we donate money back into the department. We have a small private practice where we bill compensable patients. But we don't bill as individuals, we bill as a group practice. Part of this we use to pay the hospital a facility fee, part of it is invested back into the department to pay for research, education, projects, maintenance and refurbishment and equipment and then the rest of it*

is divided up in an equal and transparent way across the group. With the money that goes back into the department, we do things that we would not otherwise have the funding to do. In a world of tight funds where you only receive money for the essential things required to do the job, we are able to remain at the leading edge by providing additional equipment and services. For instance, we now have eight Intensivists here who are Harvard trained in simulation. We run simulation scenarios for all sorts of things, developing and refining both our technical and non-technical skills. To do that, we need to have the simulation mannequins, which can cost up to $100,000 depending on the complexity. Investing money back into the department allows us to buy the mannequins we need to do the training required for us to develop our skills and improve our performance. Echocardiography, the use of ultrasound to assess the heart, is used more and more, and now more than half our group are qualified echocardiography practitioners. These funds have enabled us to purchase the latest whizz bang machine.

Intensive care is a high tech and expensive area in which to work. Carlos believes that investing money back into the department is beneficial, and everyone has the incentive to do.' We can then provide the individuals in the group with the latest technology to be able to do the best they can for our patients, in their particular area of interest'.

The next initiative Carlos set up was the introduction of external courses. 'We run a Harvard style postgraduate education program here. Every year we run 32–33 courses externally. Every couple of weeks we have at least one course running. We specialise in those areas in which we believe we have special expertise, such as renal, mechanical ventilation, bronchoscopy, echocardiography, and Extra Corporeal Membrane Oxygenation. These courses also bring in income, which all goes back into the department. None of it goes to the individuals, but it means that they have the means by which they can progress and develop in their particular areas of interest'.

Carlos discussed the various benefits of investing money back into the department.

> *It all goes back into the department, so no one has any particular problem with it. At the end of the day, the unit is better because we actually chip in for the things that the hospital would otherwise be unable to fund. The other benefit of the courses is that everyone works together to develop and run the courses, which improves the teamwork within the group. Teaching on the courses also improves the individuals' clinical skills making them better at the bedside, and it also assists in 'branding' the hospital and the Alfred ICU as a centre of excellence.*

There was a secondary by-product that Carlos could never have predicted when he first set out on this journey. 'Another positive is that because our education program is so good, it attracts people here. We've got people waiting to come and work here. Whereas many places are having difficulties in getting staff, I'm full. This creates two problems. The first is that for the junior doctors in training, there is now a wait list of two years and the nursing staff are also put on a wait list to work here. If we put an ad out for jobs, we'll have a lot of people applying'. Not a bad position to be in. The other consideration for Carlos is his low turnover rate. On the one hand it's fantastic to have a well-established team running at a thousand miles an hour, the downside is that according to McKinseys, you're supposed to have a third of your staff in the lower tier, a third in the middle and a third in the top. Carlos was quite introspective on this issue. 'That's a problem for me. I'm all out of kilter because so few leave. We are very top heavy. The majority of our nurses are in the top tier, which is good because highly experienced staff contribute to our really good patient outcomes. However, the price of that is that we have a very senior and very expensive workforce'.

The question I am sure many of you are considering is: how do you then bring someone new into this well-functioning team? It is likely that any new recruit is going to experience a sense of anxiety about their performance far beyond the normal, simply due to the high performing nature of the team. Carlos recognises that it is unlikely he will find talent who will fully hit the ground running. 'By definition, because we are unique in the provision of the variety of State Services and the complexity of our case mix, no one would have seen all of these unless they've worked here. Most external people would have only experience in some of these areas. I start off with the principle that no one new is going to know everything that we do, so we are going to have to teach them about some of our specialties'.

> *The cultural fit of an employee to an organisation is critical to their satisfaction and productivity, and is something Carlos considers extremely important. What I'm interested in is their cultural fit, fitting into this group of high achieving, hardworking people that work together and that help each other out. I can give you a million examples. The other day, I had one person rostered on for night shift but it was so busy that there were four consultants here still at midnight helping (and without*

*additional pay). The way the group works together is
fabulous and that in turn creates a special culture in the
place. I don't tell people that they have to answer emails
at 3 am in the morning, but they do have to be a person
who's going to fit into the culture, a culture of wanting
to achieve, wanting to be the best, and wanting to work
together. That's what's important for me when interviewing
and hiring new people.*

Carlos then explains the importance of hiring right the first time, which, in turn, will make it easier to motivate and have a positive and successful workforce. 'If you start off with the right people, they're really easy to encourage and motivate. They're not getting paid as much as a lot of Intensivists in other units, but I think they have a lot more job satisfaction than most others. My role here is therefore to make sure that I create the right atmosphere for everybody to be able to flourish'.

There is a school of thought that suggests you need one major thing:

The right people with the right mindset doing the right work.

But what happens if you don't? Maybe a better question is how do you ensure that you stay ahead of the performance management curve and catch problems before they create major issues in your business? Carlos decided to utilise an intense form of 360-degree evaluations, which involve receiving feedback from all the people one works with (e.g.

manager, peers, and direct reports). While this is a common form of evaluation and monitoring in organisations, the development of the 360 in Carlos' department is particularly unique.

> *All of my specialists have a 360 yearly. When we started this, they all got together and devised the 360. They created the questions regarding what was important in their jobs and what was expected of them. We then together created the list of people to whom the questions would go. As a result, we are all evaluated by the entire peer group; the junior doctors, the nursing leadership and about 120 specialists in the rest of the organisation with whom we deal on a regular basis. I outsource this list to a market research company who puts it all online, collates it and issues a report. Every year, it now automatically goes out to every single person on that list. Not all respond, but on average, every member of the team receives feedback from more than 50 people. It therefore is unlikely to be biased, one-way or another. I am at arms length, no one gets to pick to whom it is sent, the group does that, and the questions were all made by the group.*

What is unique about Carlos' department is the transparency under which the monitoring and feedback operates. 'They [the staff] know that there is feedback coming, and everybody deals with their feedback. If you don't deal with or are unable to address the feedback, we put in whatever supports are needed to assist the individual to deal with it. If you haven't improved by the next time around then there is a problem of fit; this isn't the right place for you or you are not the right person for this place. Everybody understands before they have even started that they will be evaluated according to this process and are expected to do well'. The outcomes of such a process have evidently been successful. 'When we started it, we had an expectation that everybody would score in the top third. It's now in the top 25 per cent. The overall score for the department when you add up all the individuals was 90 per cent for 2014'.

Having utilised 360-degree evaluations in a number of consulting programs, the one phrase I am continually having to deal with is the "Yes, but". This is best translated into 'Yes I have read the feedback from my peers, but here is why it is wrong or has been misinterpreted'. The overall outcome is usually the individual minimising the feedback and making very little change in their behaviour. Carlos's group is well beyond this. 'This group has passed the "yes, but". If you're a "yes, but" you're not getting the whole process. I don't think the group is motivated by the desire not to fail. When you talk to the junior staff at the end of their rotations, the comment they all make is that this is such a great group. Everyone strives for the best, and we work really hard at being the best group, having the best patient outcomes, being the best at teaching and research'.

In addition to his intense feedback program, Carlos is also a big fan of using mentors as a way of guiding his staff. 'The senior doctors in training are here for at least a year or two. At the more junior level they will rotate for 3 or 6 months as part of their training'. To make induction easier, Carlos' team introduced a mentoring structure.

> *Any new senior consultant is mentored by either me or one of the deputies. All of the consultants will mentor one of the senior registrars, all of the senior registrars mentor a junior registrar, the nursing leadership mentors the new senior nurses and new nursing staff going into the unit are*

allocated someone to mentor them as well. We have a very well developed mentorship program in the department that tries to make the transition as smooth as possible. It also makes clear what the expectations are, so that there is no mismatch between expectations and performance.

Bringing Innovation to a High Performing team

In line with the team's mission statement and desire to continually move the team forward, Carlos expanded on his approach to opening communication between his team members. 'We all sit down as a group every week for three hours and have a meeting with all the consultants and nurse managers. All of the senior registrars are invited to attend. That meeting goes through mortality, morbidity, and problems in the areas we need to work on. All of the key things that happen in the department go through that particular meeting. The meeting therefore identifies all sorts of areas of need'. At one of these meetings a particularly important discussion was held relating to the ongoing challenge of communicating with relatives.

Relatives are distressed, and it is a very high stress time for them. You tell them things but they don't necessarily hear it the way you've said it, or they forget it. So we developed an iPad app. We now have six iPads in the reception area that tell you all about ICU: what to expect, the noises you hear, the equipment you see, the procedures we do, the risks of the procedures, hotels nearby, where to eat, where to stay, public transport, etc. We won the Australian mobile and app award for 2014 in the medical division for this.

Driving innovation is difficult at the best of times, it's hard enough to come up with ideas, let alone actually bringing them to completion. For any organisation or department to be disruptive they need to have a culture that allows for innovation and a leader that will support and drive the process. This is a no-brainer for Carlos; innovation is built into his psyche and subtly into the mission statement and for that matter almost every single activity his group partakes in. For Carlos the concept of innovation is simply a way of operating – not only could he not recall who came up with the App idea, I don't think he particularly cared. For him the process was far more important and the outcome achieved a goal that benefitted the team. 'Somebody came up with the idea, and then the group came together, and added a few things. It's just a fabulous app and something we are all very proud of. It is having up to 3,500 screen views per day'. Once he got started on thinking about all the wonderful ideas his team had there was no stopping him. 'There is a whole range of new, innovative things we get into. Let me give you some other examples:

» We've got our own website, which is independent of the hospital. We advertise all of the courses through it, and a whole range of information is available on the website. It is getting more than 100 hits a day. It is instrumental in attracting staff to our department and communicating with relatives and both internal and external parties.

» One of the new guys with particular skills in social media has set up a blog for educational purposes. He sent me the stats yesterday. It's about one year old today; it has 1,800 followers on twitter, and is getting up to 800 hits a day: only 25 per cent are from Australia, the rest are from 159 different countries.

» When you have heart surgery, you go onto bypass, and there is a machine that takes blood out from the heart, oxygenates it, and pumps it back. A long time ago, we started doing this in the ward, to support the heart and lungs. We are now probably one of the leading groups in the world using this particular technique. We set up a new model of care involving going out, putting patients on this and retrieving them here, which won a Victorian public healthcare award. We are now pretty slick at this. Earlier this year, there was an Australian who got sick and ended up on one of these machines in Japan. We went to Japan, changed him over to all our equipment, picked him up and dropped him off in Queensland where he lived and came back home.'

These consistent successful achievements create a high morale amongst Carlos' team. 'All of this constantly feeds back to the group to continue the high morale'. This is a result of the 'We can do anything' mindset.

Throughout the interview, Carlos continually referred to his high performing team and the concept of 'we can achieve anything' was well re-enforced. He didn't waiver from this position and never referred to a specific individual that had achieved something remarkable.

Yes. It is not the recognition of an individual. It is the group. Whilst there are a lot of people here who are experts in their field and are highly regarded, it is the group that does it. By working together, they enable the individuals to do what they do. But the individuals couldn't do it without the support of the group. Last year, the group achieved excellent patient outcomes, more than $5 million in research funding, produced 145 publications, and taught 1,150 participants through its highly regarded education program as well as receiving numerous awards. It goes to the concept of the superior team, where you achieve extraordinary results that are bigger than the *individual results. You compensate for each other's strengths and weaknesses.*

Interacting with the wider organisation

The final piece to Carlos's puzzle is how to ensure his team interacts with the wider hospital group. There is always a risk that a highly successful team can without any real desire create their own silo simply as a by-product of their success. You can imagine a situation in which other departments look at what is being achieved and react to the success. Reaction to other people or companies success has always been a fascination of mine, we see some aspects of incredible support and reverence for success, but then just as quickly we see the tall poppy syndrome kicking in. There is often no pre-cursor to the response and it is usually an emotional one hence the ambiguity in understanding it. Carlos recognised the potential for this and ensured that the risk was minimised.

Part of the emphasis is that we didn't want to be a silo. We wanted to integrate into the wider group and have a role in the wider group. My team currently sits on 30 committees within the organisation and about 60 external committees. The benefit is that anything that happens gets our input and we know what is happening. In turn, it means that we can position ourselves and make sure we take advantage of the situation. We can ensure we change course so that we're aligned with the organisation and everything heads in the right direction. That's really important. Part of the committee involvement was in order to build bridges with the rest of the organisation and to improve relationships. Because of these improved relationships and due to our large involvement within the organisation, we can actually take part in a whole range of things that happen within the organisation.

This approach has improved his team's relationship and led to greater involvement of the ICU team within the organisation.

At the moment, there's a new way that the hospital runs at night. Traditionally, fairly junior people worked independently in the hospital at night. About two years ago, the organisation created a new position called the clinical lead. The clinical lead is the most senior of the doctors in training on site overnight, sits on top of all of the junior medical staff and coordinates them, making sure there is some teaching so that it is not just a task oriented night. They are also responsible for load levelling. It's all about progression of care, ensuring that nothing stops because it's night time, and that the night works as well as, or better than the day. When all of that was happening, the natural group to take on the role of clinical lead was the senior registrars from ICU because they were the most senior people, they were the best equipped to deal with critically ill patients and if anything went wrong, they had the respect of both the surgical and medical teams, who would listen to them. This is an example of how we have aligned ourselves with the needs and direction of the wider organisation. Our relationship with the rest of the organisation is actually pretty good. We are not at odds with the place. We are working well with and are aligned with the organisation.

Sometimes you just get it right, but like the saying goes, behind every great team is a great leader – or something like that. Carlos found his teams operating rhythm and stuck to his mantra 'It all starts with a clear vision'.

Carlos shared his mission statement with me and it follows this paragraph. It is important to remember that you can't simply copy someone else's mission statement and hope it will work for you. But you can explore how others have achieved their goals and then reflect on your situation in developing a statement that captures the sentiment of your business and the goals you are trying to achieve. Take some time to read this statement and consider if your companies mission statement truly reflects its goals. If you don't have one, maybe you can use this as inspiration to start the process

DEPARTMENT OF INTENSIVE CARE MISSION STATEMENT

As intensive care specialists, our primary responsibility is to provide safe, appropriate, high quality care and comfort to all Alfred patients with any form of critical illness and to support those that care for them.

» **Clinical care:** Our aim is to provide best possible patient outcomes through the practice of excellent, evidence-based, compassionate and consistent team-oriented intensive care medicine. In every situation, the wishes of the patient and the hopes of those around them will be balanced with the likelihood of success and suffering. Our practice will include dignified end-of-life care if treatment becomes futile.
» **Communication:** To keep our patients and their relatives well informed. To communicate effectively with our colleagues and other hospital staff.

- » **Support:** To build positive relationships within and outside our department. To support our colleagues in our clinical and academic pursuits so that we can attract, inspire, and nurture diverse and committed staff that wish to continually improve their skills and knowledge.
- » **Teaching:** To facilitate critical care teaching of all intensive care and hospital staff. We wish the Alfred to be the premier place for Intensive Care training in Australia.
- » **Research:** To maintain the Alfred Intensive Care as an international centre of excellence in research. To encourage and support a broad range of research activities. To present regularly at critical care conferences nationally and internationally.
- » Management: To deliver best-practice, cost-effective responsible intensive care with wise management of human and material resources.
- » **Quality Assurance:** To continually improve our performance by regular review of all aspects of service so that we change our strategies if required. To set both long and short-term goals on an annual basis which we strive to accomplish by working together.
- » **Values:** To apply the following values to all aspects of our work: compassion, honesty, commitment, respect of personal beliefs and differences. To remain open-minded to new ideas and approaches.

TAKE HOME

- » Take your time, start slowly and gain momentum. Once you are moving, people will either get on the bus or choose to leave.
- » Feedback is essential and it needs to be broad and open. 360-degree feedback needs to all encompassing if you are going to do it.
- » Find the greater purpose for your team and you may be surprised how quickly 'selfishness' disappears.

» You are only as good as the 'worst' interaction with another part of the business. Be careful you don't create a high performing silo.

» Diverse thinking is essential, open plan offices are only as good as the planning that goes into the seat allocations. Having likeminded seated together achieves very little.

» Share your success globally, great way of building your brand.

» Actually meet with your team and make the meeting valuable. Be clear in your agenda and stick to it.

» Even the best performers need to understand your business when they join, take the time to induct your new recruits effectively.

GILLIAN LARKINS
Chief Financial Officer – Perpetual Ltd

Gillian Larkins joined Perpetual as Group Executive Transformation Office in October 2012, and assumed the role of Chief Financial Officer in January 2013.

Gaining 20 years of experience in finance, strategy and management roles across a number of industries. Most recently, she was Chief Financial Officer, Managing Director of Westpac Institutional Bank, responsible for Finance and Strategy, and prior to that, Chief Financial Officer Australia and New Zealand of Citigroup. Gillian has also served on the board of Hastings Fund Management as a non-executive director from 2009 to 2011.

As a member of the Executive Leadership Team reporting to the CEO, Gillian heads Perpetual's Finance, IT, and Risk functions, which include Audit, Legal and Company Secretariat.

Gillian holds a Master of Business Administration from the Macquarie Graduate School of Management, as well as a Graduate Diploma in Accounting and Finance and a Bachelor's Degree of Commerce, majoring in Economics, both from the University of Otago, New Zealand. She is a member of the NZ Chartered Accountant's Society and a Graduate of the Australian Institute of Company Directors.

A PERSONAL JOURNEY

'How do you feel the team performed during that exercise?' That was the question I had just proposed to the group as a gateway into what was to become a very robust discussion. Before anyone in the group could answer, including the CEO, Gillian raised a finger, caught the attention of the group and said, 'Thank you for the exercise, but I want to let everyone know that I was not happy with my performance or effort'. She explained that even though this was the first time she was chairing this type of meeting and the content was new to her she was not happy with her performance and identified several specific areas she would be reflecting on. In all my years of discussing the concept of 'ownership of error' this was the first time I had seen it in action and delivered with a sense of confidence and dare I say enthusiasm. I later discovered that it came from a raw and deeply held belief that continual improvement was the only path forward Gillian would accept.

Gillian, a native Kiwi (New Zealander) is currently the Chief Financial Officer for Perpetual Limited, an independent and diversified specialised investment management company, offering wealth advice and corporate fiduciary services to individuals, families, financial advisors and institutions. As an organisation they have a passion for protecting and increasing their clients' wealth. Gillian's role is vital to this success. She was quick to point out that her duty as CFO is not the traditional one and that while she is accountable for the strategic financial health and performance of the organisation, her role is somewhat larger. 'I'm fortunate enough to have a role that covers more than just numbers, in that I have the chief technology officer, the chief risk officer and the general counsel reporting to me'. Gillian explains the multidimensionality of her work. 'At any given point I can be working with numbers, listening to the latest litigation report, walking into an M and A (merger and acquisitions) meeting, or working with a technology team'. She has achieved remarkable success in her career and on reflection attributes much of her drive and motivation to her upbringing.

All of the previous chapters explored the approaches taken by the individuals to achieve success in their current roles. This chapter will take a slightly different angle as we explore how Gillian traversed the corporate ladder and found success. It is important to remember that our journey to a point is just as important as the actions we take right now. As much as we don't like to recognise it, we are a product of our past and almost every experience we have will in some shape or form influence our reactions and behaviours. For many of us, this is inconsequential and we don't pay attention to why we act in a certain way and very often only reflect on what we just did. After many years of working with elite athletes and corporate executives, the characteristics of self-reflection and proactive insight (that is, reflecting on what we did and deliberately trying to understand why we did it) appear to be paramount in the prediction of future success. The ability to understand 'why' and then choose to do something about it (good or bad) is vital. I often reflect on 'why' I became a psychologist and ironically it wasn't until about ten years after graduating that I actually got the answer.

Gillian was clear on how her journey started. 'My dad wanted to ensure that I had an education and a profession that I could fall back on. At that time, accountancy was closely related to business and fortunately, after starting the course I realised that I actually enjoyed it and even came to love it'. Having the ability to do math in her head I suspect also made it easier for Gillian, as the concepts made sense. After graduating she trained at Ernst and Young and then at age 25 moved to London. Moving from a small country like New Zealand to make it big in London, sounds like your typical romantic movie, picture Tom Hanks standing on top of the Empire state building waiting for the love of his life, Meg Ryan, to appear. I am sure that many people have thought about doing this and perhaps some have even tried but not everyone has succeeded. I asked Gillian why she thought she was successful in her endeavours and like all the other points she made she was clear and on-song with her answer, 'I always set myself a clear picture of the goal I want to achieve'. This is not an approach that she had just conceptualised.

In my late teenage years, I worked out that I wanted to see as much as I could of the world and in my twenties experiment with my career options so that by my thirties I knew exactly what I was doing. During my thirties I planned to consolidate so that by my forties my ultimate goal would be achieved. As I look back now I realise that I am a very huge planner. I'm clear that there are certain points in your life where you can play, look around and move from job to job but eventually you have to start focusing and narrowing in and that has helped me with my career.

When we consider the motivation to succeed mindset, one of the key characteristics is the focus on 'mastery of the task, whilst being planned and goal oriented'. Listening to Gillian explain her mindset it is easy to see how this approach worked. However, it is one thing to set goals but a completely different task when attempting to actively pursue them.

Gillian was adamant that once she had set her goals nothing was going to stop her. An important point to remember is that the setting of goals is only the first step, the mindset of 'having a go and learning from your mistakes' is still a fundamental ingredient needed to succeed. For Gillian this started in London.

I landed at Morgan Stanley and accepted a locum role. Between the age of 25 and 29, I travelled around Europe fixing stuff. I learnt about Europe, about the bigger world, and that even though accounting was my training, there was a lot more that could be done with it other than debit or credit. That job gave me an understanding of how to learn and to problem solve. Afterward, I worked with the Boston Consulting Group where I honed my consulting skills and how you can be more strategic with numbers. During my twenties I was discovering what I wanted to do. When I was 29, I was with KPMG corporate finance doing valuations, and then I decided to move to Sydney. There, I ended up working at Woolworths for four years providing strategic planning. I finally understood how to be a strategic CFO and how to realise strategy through numbers.

There is a consistent theme coming through with Gillian's experience and it is one of 'continual learning'. Each situation she found herself in created a whole new challenge and broadened her armoury of skills. I asked her if she defines herself as an accountant given her initial training, her response was, 'I am a problem solver more than I am an accountant'. It is important to recognise that while your training may have given you a title, it will not give you a career; that is still up to you and the choices you make.

We all have times when we have choices to make that take courage to follow through on. In an earlier chapter, I defined courage as the ability to make a commitment without any guarantee of success. Consider the last time you were given an opportunity and you weren't sure how it would turn out; on which side of the continuum was your mindset when you actually made the decision? Gillian, without the knowledge of the motivational continuum, found herself in this exact position after returning to Australia. 'I applied for a job at Citigroup to be the head of planning, but instead I was offered the role of CFO at the investment bank. I had no idea why they offered it to me'. Gillian discusses going home to her husband in disbelief and unsure of her ability to do the job, to which he replied, 'What have you got to lose? What is really the worst that can happen? If you fail, it's not really a fail. You have a great opportunity to learn'. Gillian tells how since then, those words have been her mantra. 'So I went into Citigroup at 32 as the CFO of the investment bank. By 34 or 35 I was the group CFO'. This decision took her down a slightly different path than what she imagined but also opened her eyes to other opportunities. 'I realised when I was around 37 that I didn't want to go back offshore so I accepted the role offered by Westpac to be the CFO of the institutional bank'. Gillian found herself at a crossroad and with the global financial crisis looming she decided to stay and work in Australia. The financial crisis provided a natural correction for many psyches in the corporate arena. It highlighted those companies that were capable of performing under pressure, as well as the ones that were possibly punching above their weight. It is evident that when faced with the possibility of catastrophic failure the motivational mindset is truly tested. It also presented the perfect opportunity for some individuals to reflect on their careers and determine how the next phase would play out. Gillian recalls becoming somewhat demotivated during this time. 'I found that I was the fixer or the problem solver, but the people at the top of me were getting the kudos for that. There came a point where I didn't want to be 'Miss Fix It'. I have a real view about being a woman in a man's world. You have to get yourself out of that rut because women are taken advantage of sometimes. I saw myself falling into that trap so I resigned'. Within weeks Perpetual called, asking for her help in transforming the company. Gillian asserted 'Within six weeks I was given my current role and I've been doing that for nearly three years. I have had the most amazing career but it has definitely been driven by me'.

Hindsight is a wonderful tool when it comes to understanding how we made decisions in the past and what our motivations were. The greater challenge is how we apply those insights into our day-to-day actions. Gillian acknowledged this difficulty and commented that even though she was incredibly focused as a young woman, it was much clearer looking back now and connecting all the dots. Recalling our past and capturing the learning moments is a wonderful strategy to have and use especially if you are finding yourself in the motivation to avoid failure mindset. Gillian shared some incredible personal insights around her upbringing and how through the eyes of her father she developed a mindset to 'seek out, question and push myself'. Her dad was orphaned at an early age and fortunately was brought up in a nurturing environment, which ultimately led him to becoming an Olympic cyclist. She reflected that during her younger years: 'He impressed upon me the need to do things for myself. He came back from the Olympics with no education, went to night school and ended up owning his own engineering firm. From a very early age, every time I came home from school he asked me what I learnt for the day. I even do it now when I go home; I ask myself what I learnt today. It was instilled in me from a very early age'.

Always explore. Be independent. No one else is going to do it for you. You really have to drive yourself.

Having a history is not unique we all have one; some good and others less impressive. However, the broader question is, what can you do with everything you have learnt? Traditional learning through school and tertiary institutions is important and from Gillian's perspective, 'Education without a doubt is the most important gift you can have. Learning is your ticket to success'. The natural progression to learning is sharing and teaching. But this isn't as easy as it sounds. 'I think there comes a point in your career where you have a brand. It's a beautiful thing not to have when you are young'. Gillian expounded on this and stated that after reaching a certain age having this brand means that people will focus on your actions and words. 'People actually care about what you say, when you get angry, when you don't, when you smile at a function or when you don't. Unfortunately for me, I'm realising that freedom is not mine anymore. In your thirties you usually lack a profile, as a result you have more freedom to take risks. Later on you have less freedom to do that'. What Gillian is trying to say is that your brand is important, it can have a huge impact on those around you and as someone once said to Spiderman, 'With great power comes great responsibility'. Recognising the impact you have on others has been thoroughly discussed in the earlier chapters but it is vital that you understand this last point and take it on board. Just trying to cast a long 'shadow of leadership' is fraught with danger if you do not understand who you are and why you act or think in a certain way. The motivational mindset highlights and emphasises the importance of recognising the individual differences in people and that your actions will impact each of them differently.

Gillian has a very focused approach to working with her team and uses her brand effectively. Her starting point is, in her words to, 'Always have the best people around you and if possible hand pick your team'. She was very cognisant of the times in her career when she had to make the hard decision to let people go. 'It's incredibly tough, but part of leadership is making those decisions. I needed to have highly motivated teams around me and having the right people in the team actually freed up my time, allowed me to be more effective and actually helped them as well, as they were being held accountable for their own success'. She describes her current team as seasoned professionals. 'I have a very street-smart savvy team, which means in the last year I've been able to be more strategic. I have been able to start developing a different leadership style; which is leading through others, whereby I'm not doing the doing. I'm really glad I've done all the hard work and know how to do it, because I think that at this stage I deserve to stand back and allow my team to function'. It would be remiss of me not to share my private insight into this concept. I have been known to refer to this as the Elsa phenomena. To explain further, Elsa is a fictional character from the movie *Frozen* and the theme song from that movie, which has irritated millions of parents around the world was aptly called:

'Let it Go'

I must admit Gillian laughed when I explained this to her but she agreed and expanded on how this approach has supported her goals. 'I'm absolutely doing that and just as important, I am encouraging my leaders to own their space; "Own it". You're the chief risk officer or the chief technology officer, so you own that space. No one else in the company does that but you'. If Disney wants a follow up hit to their *Frozen* song it should be titled:

'Own it'

Gillian paused for the next moment reflecting on the 'own it' comment.

Her leadership style is evolving and she is very cognisant of the changes that are occurring. As leaders we need to recognise that as we grow and develop within our roles and our leadership shadow becomes longer, our style and operating rhythm needs to adapt.

> *I'm really trying to push them to the forefront. As a leader, you want other people to perform. I firmly believe that what goes around comes around. I also firmly believe in looking after people; if you do the right thing by them, they'll do the right thing by you. I must say that they are becoming better and better because they know I have their back and that they can come and talk to me about anything. At the end of the day they own their space, and it's an absolute pleasure as a leader when you see people owning their space.*

Being at the forefront is something Gillian relishes and she recognises the characteristics that others who are successful have.

> *The inspiring people I've come across have had one ingredient: authenticity. At the end of the day, they were themselves. They weren't trying to be anyone else. When you can be authentic and be yourself, I find that you are far more unshackled and more passionate. It's something that I am a firm believer in; I am very authentic. However, you don't want to be authentic and cold. It's about being authentic, inspiring and getting the best out of people.*

Her passion is also underpinned by a sense of commitment to Perpetual's values and goals. 'I'm very committed to being a business partner to the business. I'm very committed to ensuring that the CEO and board look good and I'm really committed to the old age pensioners and their dividend check. I have never wavered from that'.

The final piece to the Gillian Larkins' story is covered by my favourite question. How do you deal with failure? Gillian has a very methodical way of resolving these situations.

» My very first reaction is to be calm. I become very quiet and I just want to understand what happened before I do anything else. When it is one of my team members, I take the responsibility straight away because I feel that they are my agents. I may not have done it myself but as the leader of that team, it is my responsibility. I try to figure out what the problem is. Sometimes it can take up to a day, a week or a month to work out what the problem is.

» Secondly, stakeholder management is also incredibly important. Whoever needs to know will know straight away. I'm also always ensuring that they know when we will come back to them.

» Finally we have to sort out the issue and work out how we are going to deal with it; internally or externally? Internal issues are often dealt with differently to the ones affecting the external market but I still take full responsibility. Regardless of the situation, I am always the first line of defence and the buck stops with me. Learning from an error is vital and ensuring where possible that it doesn't repeat itself is always the goal. I don't have many two or three time offenders. I've found in the past when I've used that approach that they give back so much more, having gone through the difficulties with me. We all learn together and it normally doesn't happen again. Plugging issues as a team is essential, as everyone needs to feel as though they are part of the solution.

It is quite clear that Gillian views failure along the motivational continuum squarely from the perspective of the motivated to succeed end of the motivational mindset. To her, a failure is simply a stepping stone to future success and should always be viewed as a challenge.

TAKE HOME

» Work out what you need to 'let go' of to enable you be more successful.

» Have a plan, write it down, hold yourself accountable and 'own it'.

» Take ownership of the outcome regardless. Your team needs to know you have their back.

» Let your team have own their space.

» Calmness in the face of adversity is essential, as is stakeholder management.

» Always explore, be curious and don't take no for an answer.

VICKI CARTER
Executive Director Customer and Transformation –Telstra Consumer

Vicki Carter is an astute, engaging leader who delivers enduring, commercial results through optimising raw potential in uncertain and challenging environments. Her accomplishments are characterised by executing strategy through a 'whole of system' approach and coaching of high performing teams. She is an engaging and powerful communicator known for delivering outstanding commercial outcomes.

Vicki's career spans over 25 years predominantly across financial services and more recently in technology. She is currently the Executive Director, Customer and Transformation, Telstra Consumer. Vicki has held various executive roles at NAB including Executive General Manager, Retail Bank where she was responsible for leading the turnaround of the Retail Branch network. Prior to that she was Executive General Manager, Business Operations (effectively COO for NAB Personal Banking) and General Manager, People and Culture. Vicki has also held various senior leadership roles at MLC, ING and Prudential.

Vicki is a regular speaker on leadership, coaching and transformation. Her hands-on leadership experience has been complemented by graduate studies at Deakin University. She is also a Graduate of the Australian Institute of Company Directors and has achieved Certificates 1–3 in Executive Coaching and Leadership from the Institute of Executive Coaching and Leadership.

When you meet Vicki, her ability to articulate with a sense of humility and authority is forthcoming. She is very clear about the requirements of her role. As a leader who holds customer satisfaction at the forefront of her KPIs, she is acutely aware of how the complexity of an organisation can often create its own problems, as people are focused on achieving their own goals often blind to the impact on other departments and ultimately customers. It would not be a shock to read that some internal systems and processes can often be at loggerheads with one another. All the while, it is the customer that bears the brunt of these inconsistencies, as they are often the only ones who see (and feel) the full picture end to end.

Consider how your role interacts with the end customer in your business? If you are in a role that is customer facing, the answer is simple, but those outside that part of the business would really need to think about how their roleplays a part in the bigger picture. This is world Vicki lives in.

'Bringing the lens of the customer is one of my greatest opportunities, especially when you bring people in from the wider business and their roles may feel disconnected'. In her current role at Telstra, Vicki is charged with the task of architecting the customer experience within the consumer division. Telstra has in recent years developed a significant focus on customer advocacy, so the customer experience team that Vicki leads has the opportunity to play a really critical role in developing organisational awareness and application of customer insight in design. 'The work that we're doing is focused on improving the customer experience. We have a unique vantage point from which we can see how the customer perspective should transcend everything we do. While this is not easy it provides a great opportunity to develop new ways of working in large, complex businesses. My focus at the moment is on facilitating conversations across functions to help shape different ways of tackling a problem. By bringing together various teams, we are increasing people's understanding of the impact of their policies and practices have on each other and the overall customer experience. As a team, we can then work together to apply the insights from these unintended consequences and design a new experience for customers; one that is "joined up". We are trying to create a new way of working that transcends traditional silos within the organisation'.

Having consulted to Telstra a number of times over the past decade, recently I noticed a change. At every meeting I attended, the first agenda item was an advocacy share. A team member would stand up and share positive and negative experiences they had heard about from customers to Telstra. Speaking to Vicki I was intrigued as to how such a small team could impact a large business and truly understand their customers. 'We have an opportunity to look through and across the organisation. If your role is a custodian of the customer experience, you need to experience the organisation in a way that our customers would, so you can make the right calls in terms of where you would place your effort. This is our unique contribution'.

Vicki continued on to describe the importance of having the customer's point of view in her work.

> *For me, the optimal way to do continuous improvement is through the lens of the customer, particularly if you want it to be sustainable. If you're not thinking about value creation, then invariably there will be some other levers that are forsaken. Continuous improvement through the customer experience is unashamedly commercial. What you are doing is thinking about the whole Service Profit Chain. Your people are happier because it makes it easier for them to serve your customers in a way that they prefer to, your customers are happy because the experience is easier for them, and your shareholders are happy because you have taken out duplication and waste across the system.*

So how do you drive change and transform a business when the internal process and system don't always match the customer needs while at the same time you are motivated to ensure your customers remain committed to your brand? Vicki had a simple yet elegant answer. 'There is a need to put in place an operating rhythm and a way of working that allows you to maintain that vantage point and to notice patterns in the system so you can see what's occurring rather than just being part of it'. It all sounds so simple, just keep the customers, shareholders and staff consistently happy. I think we would all understand it is not that simple. Vicki agreed. 'One of the things I've noticed over many years is that organisations condition customers to expect disappointment and we accept it as a necessary condition. What then happens is that your effort is based around managing the element of disappointment and making it better rather than thinking about the root cause. Something I ask myself is "How much time do we actually spend creating advocacy as opposed to managing detraction?"'

From Vicki's perspective, it's very easy to put a disproportionate amount of effort into curing what doesn't go well as opposed to preventing it. That's one of the classic traps that organisations can fall into. 'We need to be putting more prevention into the system, which typically means doing really good design'.

So how do leaders prevent this? Governments have struggled with these concepts for years — it is much easier to fund something when the problem has already presented itself as we can then measure the efficacy of the intervention and ultimately justify the expenditure. It is very difficult to prove something didn't happen because you have done a wonderful job of preventing it. This is exactly what Vicki has been charged to do.

Talk to your team about the dynamics that you see. Have a conversation with your team outlining what you're noticing and ask them to describe why that is occurring. You need to engage differently. One of the reasons we build failure into the system inadvertently is because in large organisations, there is a ripple effect. People do what makes sense for their business unit in isolation but fail to see downstream or upstream impacts for either a customer or another part of the organisation. Employees are not conditioned to look across or up and see the effect of their actions.

Vicki spends the bulk of her time identifying root causes and trying to tap into the different motivations that people bring to a situation. Core to her leadership is coaching.

Coaching has been an intrinsic part of my leadership for many years. I refer to it as 'the gift that keeps on giving', and there's a simple reason for that. Unless you're asking questions of people, you don't really understand their intrinsic drivers. If your people tap into their intrinsic drivers, then you are not motivating them. They are motivating themselves. I believe that the only way you can truly unlock potential and capability in people is when they believe it themselves. The most wonderful blend of leadership encompasses sponsorship and coaching. Sponsorship is telling a person that you believe in them. Coaching effectively unlocks the ability for them believe in themselves. It's a really powerful combination. So if you talk about an environment where people can succeed and where conditions are created for self-motivation, those two things are essential.

Her coaching journey began with her time at NAB. As Executive General Manager of Retail Bank, the art of coaching was instrumental in her success. I questioned Vicki as to how she is able to lead such a large group of people. 'I think it is arrogant to think of one person leading all those individuals. I had a great team and we had a philosophy and system of coaching. It occured at every level and we invested time with our people to help them become better coaches'. While coaching sounds like a simple process of having a chat and pointing out some interesting insights, in fact, it is significantly more complex and requires a special set of skills and tools to be effective. Vicki agreed.

We created an operating rhythm, and sourced tools to enable it. We made the coaching contextual. Within a branch there is a lot of customer interaction and they are typically time poor. Therefore our coaching model was a series of quick, short and sharp, 15-minute sessions with people to discuss how they were going, what they were working on, what they wanted to achieve. We used coaching to help to create a really healthy environment and mindset.

Coaching in organisations can often be viewed as the domain of just senior leaders (as they have all the power), this could not be further from the truth. Coaching can occur at all levels in the business and doesn't always have to flow downwards. Vicki agreed with the sentiment.

When I went out with one of my managers into a branch, they would coach their direct reports and I would observe them. It would not be uncommon for five of us coaching there and for a local market leader to be coaching a branch manager, a branch manager to be coaching one of his or her people, and for all of us to observe and provide feedback.

A lovely thing about it was that there was no hierarchy. Everybody in that room understood that we were all a 'work in progress'. To some degree we're all making it up as we go and we get better through practice. It didn't mean that when you were a senior leader in the organisation you knew everything that you needed to know. We can always learn and always give feedback that would help us next time. It was an engaging and very effective way of leading the team.

Vicki is very clear that the leader has a critical responsibility to provide clarity and context; to ensure the environmental conditions are set up for success. 'As the leader, my role is to facilitate and shape an environment that enables people to know what is important and why we do what we do; to know how to think through things and to know they are backed to make the right choice in the moment with a customer or colleague'. Coaching enables you to develop the skills and wisdom in your people so they are confident to do this in a sustainable way, not reliant on constant instruction and intervention.

To achieve a level of coaching proficiency, Vicki invested in becoming a fully accredited coach. All the while, she continues to practice and to continually strive to become a better coach. And while she stopped short of challenging all senior leaders out there, she did suggest that she doesn't think anyone can be a great leader without being a great coach.

So I will throw out the challenge! Are you a great coach? How are you maintaining your coaching edge?

Coaching is vital within teams but it should not only be focused on members of the team. Leaders need to recognise how they can be coached and what style of coach is most effective for their team to ultimately be successful. Leaders play many roles – coach, counsellor, instructor, performance manager – and it is critical that when they are coaching, that is in fact what they are doing. It is important to label when you are moving into or out of a coaching conversation so there is no confusion. Many leaders feel they need to tell people what to do. While in the short term that might seem efficient and at times seductive, it doesn't build capability and is not self-sustaining. Vicki shared this perspective and had some wonderful insights for corporate Australia on why coaching was important and how to ensure you are effective at it.

Firstly, we all need to continue to improve, secondly coaching allows you to embed the right tone for your business. It also ensures that people notice that you are genuinely interested and paying attention. When people come to you to ask how to do things or to benefit from your wisdom, it can be seductive and easy to move into an "I've been in this situation a hundred times before, and therefore I will tell you the answer." That is the worst thing you can do. Of course, there are times when people are truly stuck and you need to help them. However for the most part, a better conversation and a better capability build occurs if you're actually coaching. It requires you to put your ego aside. You also have to be comfortable that you don't love all the answers and you helped them find the answers.

This last piece is often difficult, as it requires significant more time to complete and a different set of skills. It requires you to be selfless. One thing I can assure you of is that the extra time spent coaching upfront will ultimately save you significant time down the track.

In the situations described above the leader has taken a proactive approach to the coaching conversation and has integrated it into the businesses operating rhythm, but in many circumstances we ourselves could consider establishing a coaching relationship to support our own goals and aspirations. Finding a coach is not as simple as firing up Google, although you will find a number of people and companies professing to have the best coaches in the world. Vicki was circumspect about the process of finding a coach and for her it all depends on the situation you are facing and whether an internal or external coach would be most appropriate.

It depends what the context is and what the person wants to get out of the coaching relationship. In all coaching relationships, the initial terms of reference discussion is really important. People confuse coaching with mentoring or counselling. You need to be clear initially about what you want to get out of the interaction and get that on the table. If a person wants help with navigation within an organisation, it can be helpful for the coach to be internal and have knowledge of that.

However, external coaches provide additional benefits, primarily they are not vested in the organisation and they are clear on their role.

From a generic perspective, I would encourage people who are seeking a coach to ensure that it is not somebody within their department. The problem with internal coaching can be confidentiality. A sense that maybe what I'm saying might be used in another way or might help people form an idea about my lack of resilience, or my capability, or whatever it may be. NAB, as part of an enterprise leadership program engaged Conversant, an international leadership development organisation, to provide senior leaders with group coaching. Through this Vicki learned a simple and elegant equation when considering your coaching opportunity.

Value = trust + tension

Coaching is real work. You are there to get something tangible out of it. Coaches that you trust must use tension to help you sit with a level of discomfort, which creates outcomes from each session. Sometimes of the dynamics seen with internal coaching is that the relationship becomes so comfortable that it starts to become more social. If it starts to lack edge and tension, then it's time to find a new coach. This tends to defeat the purpose, as we know great outcomes emerge when there is a combination of insight and tension. When you work with someone who understands this equation, it can be a really powerful thing. There's a real liberation in that. You're really using that time for you, and not to impress anybody.

But it doesn't always work and even the best leaders will have setbacks along the way. Like all of the leaders in this book Vicki is circumspect about the concept of failure, but utilises the conversant approach that there are typically one of three underlying causes – communication, character or capability.

Almost immediately Vicki clarifies this suggesting that typically character or integrity is not the cause, as most people want to do a "reasonable job". So that leaves us with mismatch on capability and communication. The consistency in this commentary is overwhelming, but unfortunately too many leaders feel that the answer is to simply motivate their people more. It is important to recognise that the individuals are in control of their own motivation. We, as leaders, can only influence by understanding what motivates people. Vicki continued.

> *If it's capability, I go through a fairly deductive process to have various fact based conversations with people. People do experience me as being direct. I find that that's the only way to really honour people. I try to always have the conversation that needs to be had, not necessarily the one that's most comfortable. Doing that in a fact based way and showing genuine care for the individual is my typical approach. I will use facts to the extent that I can because if you're having a conversation with someone about them not performing, you need to be able to demonstrate why in a way that makes sense to them. Not only when they are in the room with you, but when they leave the room as well. You need to have those direct conversations, explore whether there is a determination between both of you that the individual can get there, and then have a very clear plan around what you're both going to do to support that. In some situations, you have to tell people that they have some strong capabilities but this is not the right role for them. I've done that many times and I've seen that many times.*

Communication on the other hand is a different beast. 'When the communication breaks down, it's all about being either on track or off track with someone'. Again Vicki adopts the Conversant approach.

'Rather than saying to somebody, "This is what I think about you", the conversation I have with them is, "This is what I think you think about me". This makes for a much richer conversation because if I'm going into the conversation saying, "Here's what I think about you", I'm probably going to hold back a little bit on that, but if I make it to "This is what I think you think about me", we have to go there and we have to get into that conversation. It's a wonderful tool to bring to the surface some of the things that are maybe getting in the way.'

You may need to read that paragraph a couple of times to get your head around the concept as Vicki is using a paradoxical approach to communicating which is challenging to do, but highly effective when mastered. Another way to think about it is to consider how you ask people to comment on your ideas or suggestions. I recently completed a large innovation consultancy and among several mindset changes we implemented into the business, the biggest by far was a single statement that we encouraged all leaders to incorporate into their day-to-day dealings. They were to replace the phrase 'What do you think about this?' with 'What is wrong with this?'. This very subtle but very powerful way of changing the communication dynamics in the room.

A final coaching formula Vicki incorporates is:

Performance = Potential – Inhibitors

I find that corporate coaching spends too much time on the inhibitors, and not enough time on the 'potential' space. I've encountered many people that have carried with them a lot of baggage because people have spent time relentlessly coaching them on what they need to improve on.

They haven't had an appreciative enquiry mindset to look for things they are doing well and ways to amplify that. It sounds like a subtle difference, but it delivers a profound change.

When asked 'What do great leaders do?' Vicki identified the following points.

» Set the context (i.e., the vision) – This needs to be in a person's everyday role because it helps them make decisions.

» Clarity around expectations – Sometimes leaders lose their team if they are not clear about what success looks like.

» Aligning to purpose – People are looking for something that has meaning for them

» Composure – A leader needs to be adaptive. Particularly because your team is looking to you

» Bringing the team together – Take time to ask your team what and how they want to be.

TAKE HOME

» Keep a notebook record of all your positive encounters.

» Coach and be coached.

» Have the right conversations at the right time; it may feel uncomfortable but in the long run is more productive.

» Consider the potential before the inhibitor.

» Tension should be used in a healthy way to drive positive change.

» Your leaders still need feedback, there is no reason why it can't come from you.

» Focus on capability and communication issues, which are usually absent or mismatched when conflict or lack of trust occurs.

Final word

WAYNE HENDRICKS
Head of Global Security Macquarie Group

I hope you have enjoyed the book and considered how you might approach motivation going forward, I really wanted to end with an insight into an individual who we are glad exists and rarely gain an insight into.

Wayne Hendricks is the Chief Security Officer (CSO) of Macquarie Group and a member of the Business Resilience Steering Committee, the Cyber Working Group and the Reputational Risk Committee. Wayne was appointed CSO in 2009 and is responsible for corporate security, fraud management and intelligence. Prior to joining Macquarie, Wayne spent eight years at Goldman Sachs leading various security functions, including as head of executive protection. During this time Wayne also completed a BProc LLB degree.

Preceding his corporate career, Wayne served as an officer in several specialised units in the South African military and police services – this included domestic and foreign training in specialist urban warfare, foreign weapons and tactics, improvised explosives and devices, operational parachuting, sniper, tracking and hostage negotiation. However, most interestingly was the team leader protection detail position he held for a prominent political figure.

On the surface Wayne Hendricks looks like any regular, somewhat fit executive. He lives in New York with his wife, daughter and newly acquired son and travels the world keeping it safe for the thousands of people who work for his business. Wayne is the current head of security for Macquarie Group and previously worked at Goldman Sachs where he was head of executive protection. While that sounds quite impressive, it's not the actual focus of this conclusion. Wayne began his career in the South African Defence Force and after a 'high speed' incident involving a parachute, he moved into the personal protection space – it is here where his life took an interesting twist.

I must stress at this point that getting Wayne to share this information took some convincing, not due to any level of embarrassment, but I believe due to his own sense humility and deep respect for a man he spent numerous hours with. Even during the interview he attempted to tone down the impact he had and the position he held – I sincerely hope I have captured the essence of his experience.

His most famous client was the President of South Africa, Nelson Mandela. Wayne joined President Mandela's detail in 1994, soon after he was inaugurated as the first democratically elected President of South Africa. It was time of significant change and tension in South Africa, but was a moment Wayne will never forget. Many of his colleagues thought he was crazy for taking on the role, but for him this was the only option that made sense. 'It was never a case of "I want to serve on a president's detail" it was nothing as glamorous as that. It was a case of incidents happening along the way that pushed me there. Due to the dynamic environment, there were openings for several professionals to join President Mandela's protection detail. At that time few were interested in this job ... at least from the "old government"'. On the topic of why many of his friends chose not to work for President Mandela, Wayne explained.

> *Many of my friends looked at it and said, 'We're not going to work for Mandela, he's a communist'. Some guys would say, 'we're not going to work for him, that's a pretty high risk job, I'm sure somebody is going to take him out (assassinate) him'. Others would say, 'I want to work for president de Klerk [the president of the country at the time] as that's better from a career perspective'. I looked at them and said, 'It sounds like an adventure; it sounds like something where I can make a change' and that's how I picked it. It was as simple as that.*

One can imagine that at this time, tempers and intolerance between the white and black South African population were at an all-time high and it was no different on Mandela's detail. 'Initially it was very much us and them, us being the white protection detail (appointed by the old SA government) and them being the newly appointed African detail (appointed originally by the ANC). I think it took at least two years for us to gel as a team. It was tough going'. Wayne further explained the initial reluctance to work together as a team and how they would often protest that having had better training or better gear advantaged the white group. Or at least that was the perception. However the dynamics changed. 'The connection (between the team) comes a lot from our capabilities and the fact that we quickly developed this kind of pride factor and loyalty for Madiba.' Madiba is clan name given to Nelson Mandela, and is used as a sign of respect and admiration. 'So we would get on a shooting range or go for a run, and those guys that could really perform made it easier for us as a team because it evolved from an "us and them" to a inclusive "us". The difference became a matter of skill and not one of race. The net benefit was a team that pushed itself to be better than everyone initially expected'. Capability and teamwork became the underlying principles of the team.

So how do you get your head around the concept of putting your life ahead of somebody else's? 'I don't think anyone thinks about it that way'. Wayne went on to explain how when a president is standing on a podium, others may think, 'Wow, a sniper might shoot him', but he would focus on the small surrounding details. 'We would look at it and focus on the small details around that plan: Do the surveillance guys have complete visibility of what's around us? What is the podium's height? Are the flags drawn so the people can't anticipate the wind from 2 km away? Where is the sun sitting? I'm thinking about the next movement, so I'm trying to get the logistics right for that'. Once the details of the operational plan are being focused on, Wayne describes that there is no time to think about the fact that he may need to put his life ahead of the president's. 'Your training kicks in. If you hear a shot, you don't think, I'm going to sacrifice my life for a president. You think "I have to do the following moves in terms of our tactics to protect the president". You focus on that action or movement. Then collectively as a team, you're actually protecting the president. So I don't think anybody really thought about it'. He further reinforced the need to train effectively. 'Lessons learnt are good and enable us to reflect and learn, but remember the next event may not be the same as the previous and therefore the lessons learnt may not apply – the trick is to train, train and train'.

Wayne summed up his approach to working with high performing teams and maintains this approach has transferred seamlessly into his corporate career.

Always look for the best quality answer in the room, not the most senior person's opinion.

This way of thinking has seen Wayne transition successfully from a physical protection role to a pseudo protection role in which he is responsible for supporting Macquarie Group globally in its efforts to keep its people safe.

> *My job is not to catch a terrorist. It's to make sure that if something happens, we can assist our staff based on what we can control, and make sure that Macquarie, in a practical and realistic way, is protected. We constantly calibrate what we do according to our risk profile as an organisation, globally, and then specifically in each country. We don't need to bump up security like the MI5 headquarters in London or the Pentagon in the US. Our offices around the world are completely safe.*

To ensure he and his team are on the front foot they are continually, 'Plugged into all the forums and get intelligence from various sources, both private and government. Do we need to do anything else? No!'

Wayne now faces challenges regarding public perception of risk often fuelled by the media

> *I'm fighting the perception of risk that's given mainly by the media and to some degree by the government, which is actually a far cry in many circumstances from what the real risk is against an organisation. People get stuck on it because they don't look at that type of risk based approach. Instead, they respond – 'oh my god there is a terrorist attack, we have to do something about it.' Current low grade, franchise-style terrorism has pushed governments and intelligence agencies specifically to change their approach in terms of surveillance and ultimately preventing an attack. These days it's much harder to spot the "bad guys"... especially when we start to think about cyber terrorism.*

Wayne explains how the average person believes that 9/11 could happen again, and believes that the government is not protecting them from such an occurrence. His position is that a '9/11-style attack is significantly harder today to pull off than say in 2004. Not in the next 10–15 years. The days of "I'm a member of Al Qaeda, I have to go for training in a certain country so I have to travel before I can commit atrocity" are over. The motivational drivers of these individuals have shifted so our mindset should change from prevention, to thinking about what is actually happening at the moment'. Wayne's perspective is that the motivation to succeed mindset will allow us to stay in the present and not simply be focused on the motivation to avoid failure. Ironically, the continuum in its purest form explains why governments are so focused on not failing in the eyes of the population that they often lose sight of what is happening in front of them.

But with all of this going on around him, Wayne still needs to focus on the issues that are facing him day and day and ultimately informing his business as to matters of safety for its staff. 'We need to remember that while making money is important and vital, our people should always be at the forefront'.

> *We have a thousand incidences that range from a burst water pipe to servers going down, but 99 per cent of that never really transfers to staff safety. But if you look at what happened recently in terms of the terrorist attack in Sydney, Australia (January 2015) and Tunisia, France (June 2015), the threat is real. It's becoming more complex and if we really believe that it's about people's safety and not just about reputation and money, then we should put our money where our mouths are and make sure the decisions are first and foremost geared towards our people's safety. For me this is glaringly and acutely apparent.*

Wayne ends his point by purporting that he does not get side-tracked by whether a decision he will make is popular or not, 'Because if I dilute my thinking in terms of that, I think I'm going to be less valuable to Macquarie when we need to protect our people'.

So how does an individual like this respond to failure and create a high performing team around him driven by the same mindset. 'I am focused on my team's development, I see this as being the most important component of a high performing team'. Wayne went on to explain that everyone is different and will approach their role differently but this diversity allows him to sleep much better at night as his team effectively has five sets of eyes all looking at the ever unfolding world events with an educated but diverse perspective. 'I am confident that even if one person in my team misses a piece of valuable information, another will pick it up. We can't all be expected to be experts at everything but we can expect everyone to work together and be aligned on our set of values'. Some time ago I ran a workshop for Wayne as he had recently recruit several new members, on the surface I questioned the value I could to his team. They were a team of security experts who were highly trained and at the top of their game. But Wayne was quick to point out that as a disperse team located across the globe he wanted to ensure that they spent significant time getting to know each other and developing a team value system which would see them through the good and tough times. The team was incredibly open to the idea and recognised the value in building this ethos and determining the leadership behaviours they would hold each other accountable to.

During dinner that night I asked Wayne if he had a personal motto or a value that underpinned his approach to life and his answer was swift and precise.

Earlier I referred to my definition of the difference between good and great being *the ability to perform consistently under pressure*. It would seem Wayne has found another great way of saying it!

You only feel pressure if you don't know what you are doing.

So here we are at the end of the book and I hope you have enjoyed the read and stolen some nuggets for your personal use. I leave you with this final thought:

> *Consider how you are impacting your people, peers and the environment you operate in. Consider how you could be more effective, maybe it's time to stop motivating them!*

Part III

YOUR MOTIVATIONAL MINDSET
Building your own continuum

Consider the picture below and ask yourself how many times you accidentally catch yourself falling below the line. To remain motivated your challenge is to stay above the line and when the going gets tough you need to dig deep.

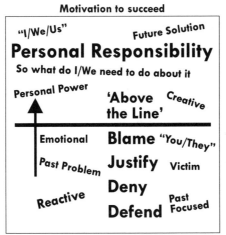

Motivation to succeed

"I/We/Us"   Future Solution
Personal Responsibility
So what do I/We need to do about it

Personal Power

'Above the Line'   Creative

Emotional   **Blame** "You/They"

Past Problem   **Justify** Victim

Deny

Reactive

Defend Past Focused

Motivation to avoid failure

Let's start with recognition. As we all respond very differently to our environment and the signs in one person are often very different in others, this is where it gets interesting. It is interesting as many of the outward symptoms are there – i.e. the behaviours, but it is the internal symptoms that differ. That is our thought processes, which are all different and the variables in your world, which trigger your shift in the continuum from MTS to MTAF mindsets will be different. Therefore we need to start with the mirror test. This is the simple test in which we look in the mirror and consider our responses to different environments and how we are able to adapt.

Start by making a list of the types of situations you find yourself in. Focus primarily on the situations in which you have an element of evaluation attached. While not all situations will develop a MTAF response, the ones that contain evaluations of any sort are more likely to do so.

Next, consider whether the event has significant importance to you. You may find events in which you are evaluated but don't perceive them to be important and therefore your responses to these events will be viewed differently to those situations perceived as important.

With that in mind, now start capturing situations that are important to you and situations in which you could be evaluated. Note that the evaluation does not have to come from an external source; you can be the source of your own evaluation.

List your situation here

_____

_____

_____

_____

_____

_____

_____

_____

Now try to consider why you are being evaluated and why it is important. This is the hard part! If you are getting stuck, head back to the section before and reconsider the why?

Getting to the why is the most important aspect of enabling your ability to shift your perspective.

Next, we need to find out which mindset is most prominent for you. Remember we will respond to both mindsets but have a higher propensity for one or the other.

COMPLETE THE MOTIVATIONAL QUESTIONNAIRE

The questionnaire should only take about 10–15 minutes to complete. I highly recommend you don't spend too much time thinking about your answer and simply answer with the first thought that comes to mind. Once you have completed it, you need to score it. The scoring formula is found at the end and you will receive two scores – a Motivation to Succeed score and a Motivation to Avoid Failure score.

MOTIVATION QUESTIONNAIRE

1	I have the ability to get my colleagues 'fired up' or motivated to achieve.
2	I have a very strong desire to be successful in my career.
3	Before a project I don't worry too much about what is going to happen.
4	Others do not see me as an outstanding worker.
5	I seem to work better when being observed.
6	Colleagues respect the way I get the small stuff done.
7	I would be willing to work additional hours in order to be a success in my career.
8	I don't find it difficult to sleep the night before an important meeting.
9	I often take a loss or unsuccessful event harder than I should.
10	I don't seem to be as mentally tough as most of my colleagues.
11	I work hard in my role in hopes of gaining recognition.
12	I am nervous and fidgety right before a presentation.
13	I enjoy having people see me perform.

Strongly Disagree 1	Disagree 2	Neutral 3	Agree 4	Strongly Agree 5
O	O	O	O	O
O	O	O	O	O
O	O	O	O	O
O	O	O	O	O
O	O	O	O	O
O	O	O	O	O
O	O	O	O	O
O	O	O	O	O
O	O	O	O	O
O	O	O	O	O
O	O	O	O	O
O	O	O	O	O
O	O	O	O	O

14	I enjoy making suggestions that will help a colleague achieve success.
15	My goal is to become outstanding in my chosen career.
16	Colleagues respect my leadership abilities.
17	It is hard for me to stay calm before an important proposal.
18	I am not pleased with my mental toughness at work.
19	I try very hard to be the best.
20	Colleagues respect my persistence and determination.
21	After an unsuccessful project, I find it difficult to sleep.
22	I usually feel butterflies in my stomach just before a presentation.
23	Sometimes when I lose or fail, it bothers me for several days.
24	When compared to someone of my own ability, I often fail more than I succeed.

O	O	O	O	O
O	O	O	O	O
O	O	O	O	O
O	O	O	O	O
O	O	O	O	O
O	O	O	O	O
O	O	O	O	O
O	O	O	O	O
O	O	O	O	O
O	O	O	O	O
O	O	O	O	O

SCORING:

To analyse the questionnaire you need to add up your scores from specific questions. Different questions make up your MTS and MTAF scores.

Your Motivation to Succeed score is made up of questions 2 + 7 + 11 + 15 + 19. Each answer is associated to a number, which can be found at the top of the questionnaire. Add up the numbers associated to each question and then capture it on the continuum below

Strongly Disagree	Disagree	Neutral	Agree	Strongly Agree
1	2	3	4	5

Your Motivation to Avoid Failure score is a little more complicated as you need to reverse the scores of questions 3(R) and 8(R) and then add your scores from question 12, + 17, and 22. Capture your score on the continuum below.

R = reverse the score. On question 3 and 8 record your score and then reverse it

1 becomes a 5	5 becomes a 1
2 becomes a 4	4 becomes a 2
3 stays the same	

Motivation to succeed score   Motivation to avoid failure score
_____   _____
_____   _____
_____   _____
_____   _____
_____   _____

MOTIVATIONAL MINDSET
Interpreting your results

Unlike other scales, a high score on this questionnaire is not good or bad, it is simply indicative of your ability to shift from one side of the continuum to another. You will also notice that you do have scores on both sides of the continuum. For those of you who are interested, I have included a copy of the test on my website which will automatically score it for you. Head to www.gavinfreeman.com navigate to the media section and click the link to books.

What do the numbers mean? In the most simple terms, the higher the number the easier it is to slip into that mindset, and vice versa. Practically speaking, if your MTAF failure score is high (for the purpose of this activity assume a high score to be in the 18–25 range) then you are more likely to shift into this mindset. Likewise, if your MTS score is high then given the context of the situation you are more likely to shift into this mindset. What does likely to shift mean? In essence, if the context is driven by a culture of failure and you have a high MTAF score, then you will shift easier and most likely feel more comfortable in this mindset.

To understand the outcome goal you would like to achieve consider the steps required to achieve it.

_____

_____

_____

_____

_____

_____

Challenge yourself on how you will respond to failure, whether it is inferred, imminent or you have actually failed. Regardless you need to determine how you used to respond and then create the ideal response.

Current reactions to failure	Future reactions to failure
_____	_____
_____	_____
_____	_____
_____	_____

The final step of the puzzle is building accountability to change. Answering these few questions may help in the process.

» Who am I sharing my goals with?
» How am I making them come to life? (sharing a goal on Facebook can actually be quite powerful)
» What mindset is driving the new goal?
» How will I know that I am reverting to my old style?
» What process will I use to re-align my goal?

Finally, always remember:

Disappointment leads to determination to improve – which creates a challenge – that requires courage to achieve – and develops greatness.

First published in 2016 by New Holland Publishers Pty Ltd
London • Sydney • Auckland

The Chandlery Unit 704 50 Westminster Bridge Road London SE1 7QY United Kingdom
1/66 Gibbes Street Chatswood NSW 2067 Australia
5/39 Woodside Ave Northcote, Auckland 0627 New Zealand

www.newhollandpublishers.com

ISBN 9781742577807

Managing Director: Fiona Schultz
Publisher: Alan Whiticker
Project Editor: Jessica McNamara
Designer: Andrew Quinlan
Production Director: Olga Dementiev
Printer: Toppan Leefung Printing Limited

10 9 8 7 6 5 4 3 2 1

Keep up with New Holland Publishers on Facebook
www.facebook.com/NewHollandPublishers